DEAD ORTHODOXY
AND
ITS CURE

Register This New Book

Benefits of Registering*

- ✓ FREE **replacements** of lost or damaged books
- ✓ FREE **audiobook** – *Pilgrim's Progress*, audiobook edition
- ✓ FREE information about new titles and other **freebies**

www.anekopress.com/new-book-registration

*See our website for requirements and limitations.

In a manner much like A. W. Tozer and the spiritual writers of the past, Ryan Denton challenges readers – especially those in conservative and doctrinally confessional churches – to again heed the call of revival by the power of the Word and the unction of the Holy Spirit. Like a modern-day Josiah, he smashes down idols, grinds up legalism, dethrones antinomianism, and stomps on formalism and the idea of promulgating "religious goods and services" in the marketplace of pragmatism. This book will hurt to read. It will confront your sensibilities. It will call you to repentance. And should you have the courage to look at your own soul in the mirror of God's Word, Denton will help you to put the pieces back together and avoid the dual errors of losing our first love while growing lukewarm in our worship.

Dr. Matthew Everhard
Jonathan Edwards scholar and Pastor of Gospel Fellowship
Presbyterian Church (PCA), Valencia, PA

I am indebted to the good hand of Providence for this enlightening and engaging work. The content was so rich and resonated so much in my heart, it is difficult to capture in two brief paragraphs the words to describe its impact on me. This book has struck a harmonious chord in my heart concerning the ever growing pragmatism in our day.

Because of the deficiency of experiential Christianity, many in the church have been victimized by extremes. We have taught our present generation to think deeply but not feel deeply. Therefore, this book affords a clarion call to motivate the conscientious reader to combat the complacency that is all too common in the contemporary church.

Don Currin

With a notable concern for souls, this book is a rallying cry to avoid the shackles of empty ritualism, mere tradition, and stagnant faith. Anyone interested in communicating the truths of Christianity in a compelling manner will find this work beneficial.

Pastor Anthony Mathenia
Christ Church, Radford, VA

DEAD ORTHODOXY
AND
ITS CURE

RESTORING POWER
TO THE SPIRITUAL LIFE

RYAN DENTON

www.presbypreacher.com

Dead Orthodoxy & Its Cure

© 2024 by Ryan Denton

All rights reserved. Published 2025.

Cover Designer: J. Martin

Editor: C. Miskimen

Aneko Press

www.anekopress.com

Aneko Press, Life Sentence Publishing, and our logos are trademarks of Life Sentence Publishing, Inc.
203 E. Birch Street
P.O. Box 652
Abbotsford, WI 54405

RELIGION / Christian Living / Spiritual Growth

Paperback ISBN: 979-8-88936-417-7

eBook ISBN: 979-8-88936-418-4

10   9   8   7   6   5   4   3   2

Available where books are sold

I would like to thank Pastor Joe Rosales of El Paso, Texas, for always preaching a felt Christ and for commending to me an experiential Christianity. Thanks also to Pastor Matthew Everhard, who took the time to comb the book and offered pertinent insights, specifically into the First Great Awakening. Thanks to my parents, who have supported, encouraged, and corrected me when needed for my entire thirty-nine years on earth. A special thanks goes out to my wife, Tasha, who has exuded the fragrance of a living Christianity from the first time we met. I especially dedicate this book to my three sons, James, Jude, and Jonah. We pray they will know Christ not in word only but also in power (1 Corinthians 4:20).

CONTENTS

INTRODUCTION

Too often, Christianity is presented as a mere set of propositions or as a philosophy of life. Although this is no doubt true, it is not the whole story. Christianity is also something to be *experienced*. Unlike the founders of other world religions, the founder of Christianity is alive and victorious, and He has sent the Holy Spirit to dwell inside every believer (1 Corinthians 3:16). How could this not produce what is otherwise known as *experiential Christianity*?

The Christian world is hungry for clear, sane, balanced, and scriptural teaching about warm orthodoxy. You could also call this *living* orthodoxy, as opposed to an orthodoxy that is dead or dry. Modern Christianity has addressed multiple topics, but regarding spiritual experience, it has been strangely quiet. Consequently, most Christians are malnourished in this area. We seem to believe that the only two options out there are radical enthusiasm on the one hand and deism and rationalism on the other. It is little wonder, then, that the average Christian is so hungry for a balanced treatment.

The purpose of this book is not to berate those whose

Christianity has grown cold and censorious or hard and sectarian, since this is a temptation for any of us. Rather, the motivation is to identify sources of dead orthodoxy for the sake of restoration and renewed vitality in the spiritual life. The purpose is to awaken what is asleep, to soften the hard edges of tribalism, sectarianism, and pride, and to point people to God since He alone can work in us *both to will and to work for his good pleasure* (Philippians 2:13).

Knowing how dry and calloused my own Christianity can be, I wrote this book primarily for myself, but perhaps it can also be useful for others, especially those whose Christianity needs to be channeled in a more vivified direction. Each chapter concludes with several study questions to be used corporately or for personal edification.

Whatever our shortcomings are at present, God is not done sculpting us into the image of His Son. This fact makes the writing of this book worthwhile, no matter how the Lord uses it. To Him alone be the glory.

CHAPTER 1

A FELT CHRIST

Something amazing is happening all over the Western world. People are studying the Bible with zest. They are evangelizing their neighbors and coworkers and warmly catechizing their children. They are committed to their churches and prayer meetings and hungry to know more about historic creeds and confessions. Their knowledge of Christ is enflaming their love for the gospel, the brethren, and the lost. Call it a resurgence or a reformation, but it is happening in cities and towns everywhere. There is a warmth of heart toward God and neighbor. Theological light is producing heat.

But something else is taking place alongside it. Some gatekeepers of orthodoxy are resisting such excitement. They are icily crossing their arms and shaking their heads. They see evangelism, prayer meetings, a longing for revival, and zeal in general as uncouth. It is undignified. It is not the way things are done around here. It is not the kind of Christianity people are used to. Why all the exuberance and passion, they wonder. Why this emphasis on heart religion if we know the proper doctrine and conduct ourselves *decently and in order* (1 Corinthians 14:40)?

WHAT IS DEAD ORTHODOXY?

To help us understand dead orthodoxy, we need to consider the following questions: What happens when we love the creeds and confessions of the church, but they have failed to make us more like Jesus? What happens when right doctrine makes us haughty, gruff, impatient, and hard? When we turn sour toward those not in our doctrinal camp? What happens when we are experts in theology but perpetual delinquents when it comes to the prayer closet? Instead of being tenderized by doctrine, causing us to be more sensitive to things of the Holy Spirit, what happens when we become self-reliant and proud because of our apparent knowledge? What happens when we love the doctrine more than the God whom the doctrine is about or when doctrine is more of an intellectual hobby than something that produces Christian affection? What happens when we become more zealous about winning other Christians to our specific doctrine or denomination than we are about winning unbelievers to the Lord?

The problem of dead orthodoxy is not confined to any one person, church, or denomination. Dead orthodoxy can exist in communities that emphasize theology and the intellect and in circles that do not. We can find it in midwestern Dutch churches and in evangelical churches of the Bible Belt. It exists in the rural Scottish isles and in cosmopolitan New York City. Dead orthodoxy refers to a person having Christ in name only. It is a form of godliness but without the attending power (2 Timothy 3:5). It is not a case of zeal without knowledge but of knowledge without proper zeal (Romans 10:2). There is a show of outward activity and skill but nothing of heart religion. Paul told Timothy to *avoid such people* (2 Timothy 3:5). That is how serious dead orthodoxy is.

This book is not meant to point fingers at others' "deadness" in contrast to our own "liveliness." To do so would be to fall into the error that some of the following chapters will address. For instance, one of the marks of dead orthodoxy is a hypercritical spirit. The Pharisees had such a spirit, as do many people today. But what about us? Do we have this spirit? Since I am confident that we all do, a better question would be where does this spirit appear? Are we hypercritical when we encounter someone's dead orthodoxy, or are we charitable, patient, tender, and sincerely grieved over such a condition? Are we puffed up about our own spiritual prowess in comparison to others' spiritual gauntness?

To avoid falling into this trap, we must first point the finger at ourselves. Where have we exhibited tendencies to deadness? To coldness? To hardness? To formalism? To theological tribalism or elitism? In what areas do we need to seek Christ's face afresh? Certainly, dead orthodoxy characterizes some churches, denominations, and people, but it undoubtedly finds a home in our hearts as well. In the words of Nathan the prophet, *"You are the man!"* (2 Samuel 12:7). Consider that first. We need to let repentance of dead orthodoxy work tenderness and warmth into our own souls first.

IS DEAD ORTHODOXY A REAL THING?

In one sense, there is no such thing as dead orthodoxy. The word *orthodoxy* presupposes right belief, and right belief assumes warmth and vitality, producing in a person a genuine growth in Christlikeness and love for God and man. As God's truth works in us, transformation takes place. This leads to more life, not deadness. But is it possible to have correct doctrine without a regenerated heart? Can one have right belief and even assent to that belief but not have a saving trust in the person of Christ? This book assumes this is not only possible but also common.

Think of the demons in the Bible. They knew the truth about

Jesus. They assented to the truth of Jesus's gospel. But they refused to trust Him. They did not love Him. They followed Him around, but they were not motivated by devotion. In fact, they hated Him precisely because they knew His gospel to be true (James 2:19; Matthew 8:29). Saving faith requires knowledge, assent, and trust in the gospel. But in the case of dead orthodoxy, trust can be absent. The person may be unregenerate. They may honor God with their lips, but their heart is far from Him (Matthew 15:8). The devils believe God is one and tremble (James 2:19) and so do many hypocrites.

But that is not the only explanation of dead orthodoxy. Is it possible to be a Christian but have an inconsistent outworking of that faith in one's life? Here, too, we must answer yes. All of us experience that. Anytime we sin as Christians, are we not acting inconsistently with our belief in God, our love of God, and with our hatred of sin? This is a phenomenon known as *practical atheism.*[1] We are not atheists, but our actions can indicate differently. Sanctification assumes there is an ongoing work of grace taking place within each believer, but it also assumes inconsistencies are still present. Otherwise, there would be nothing left to sanctify.

These inconsistencies can be either doctrinal or practical. Inconsistent Christian living can lead to dead orthodoxy. For example, a disappointing experience in the charismatic world can lead Christians to become skeptical of anything experiential, enthusiastic, or abnormal, which leads to an imbalance toward coldness and formalism. In the same way, an unpleasant experience with evangelism could lead to a disgust for it. Thus, the term *dead orthodoxy*, while in some ways imperfect, is a fitting description of the condition this book will address.

---

1   Stephen Charnock (1628–1680) used this term in his work on the existence and attributes of God. He was an English Puritan preacher.

A RETURN TO THE OLD PATHS

This book is not calling for something new. It calls for a return to something ancient and well within the bounds of orthodoxy. For example, the "Westminster Confession of Faith" (1647) is a document rich with experiential language. It speaks of God's withdrawal of His Spirit and God's reviving through that same Spirit (18.4). The prominent theologian William Ames, writing in the early seventeenth century, said, "Theology is the doctrine, or teaching, of living to God." He did not say theology is merely doctrine or teaching. He said it is that, but we should expect such doctrine to produce a living to God. The Heidelberg Catechism (1563) is just as clear on this point. Referring to the new birth, question 90 asks: "What is the quickening of the new man?" The answer is replete with experiential vocabulary: "Heartfelt joy in God through Christ, causing us to take delight in living according to the will of God in all good works." Unlike Ames's answer, but not inconsistent with it, the idea of *heartfelt joy* and *delight* is introduced into this notion of right living. The "Westminster Shorter Catechism" (1646) says the chief end of man is not only to glorify God but also "to enjoy Him forever," which clearly requires the affections or emotions of a person as it relates to their idea of God.

Historically, right doctrine is not just meant to be intellectual. It is to be experienced and tasted. It is to produce something inwardly and work change outwardly. This is why David exclaimed, *Oh, taste and see that the LORD is good!* (Psalm 34:8). It is what led Paul to say, *God's love has been poured into our hearts through the Holy Spirit who has been given to us* (Romans 5:5). The dry, hard, stale, non-experiential type of Christianity evidenced today in certain pockets of the Christian world is an aberration from our English Puritan, Scottish Covenanter, and Magisterial Reformed forefathers. They knew nothing of cold and clinical Christianity.

But more importantly, it is an aberration from what we see in the Scriptures. For example, white-hot orthodoxy is the norm in the Scriptures, not the exception. It blisters across the Bible from Genesis to Revelation. Abraham's faith in God led him to risk daring expeditions across unknown terrain. It ignited him to offer his son as a sacrifice, and it is what led him to send his servant to fetch a wife for that same son. Abraham's life was marked by a holy zeal for God. He was a man marked by communion with God. Abraham's God is a felt God, not a philosophical proposition. This same idea prompted Blaise Pascal to say on the night of his conversion in 1654: "From about half past ten at night until about half past midnight, FIRE. God of Abraham, God of Isaac, God of Jacob – not of the philosophers and scholars. Certitude. Certitude. Feeling. Joy. Peace."[2] Pascal's notion of God went from being an academic exercise to something tangible, alive, and teeming with heat.

We find this same fire in the last book of the Bible, Revelation, where angels, elders, and every creature in heaven, on earth, under the earth, and in the sea are unified in their delirious praise of the Lamb:

Then I looked, and I heard around the throne and the living creatures and the elders the voice of many angels, numbering myriads of myriads and thousands of thousands, saying with a loud voice,

"Worthy is the Lamb who was slain,
to receive power and wealth and wisdom and might
and honor and glory and blessing!"

And I heard every creature in heaven and on earth and under the earth and in the sea, and all that is in them, saying,

---

2   Blaise Pascal (1623–1662), an influential French mathematician, theologian, inventor, and author, wrote extensively on religion at the end of his life.

"To him who sits on the throne and to the Lamb
be blessing and honor and glory and might forever
and ever!"

And the four living creatures said, "Amen!" and the
elders fell down and worshiped. (Revelation 5:11-14)

The Old Testament prophets, especially Elijah, the gutsiest of them all, shared these sentiments. Elijah confronted King Ahab, even when he knew Ahab would delight in nothing more than to kill him. Ahab called Elijah a troubler of Israel, but Elijah retorted: *"I have not troubled Israel, but you have, and your father's house, because you have abandoned the commandments of the Lord and followed the Baals"* (1 Kings 18:18). Elijah confronted 450 prophets of Baal, even at a time when Baal worship was at its height. Afterward, Elijah challenged the people: *"How long will you go limping between two different opinions? If the Lord is God, follow him; but if Baal, then follow him"* (1 Kings 18:21).

But what gave Elijah such boldness? It was not mere orthodoxy. It was a felt orthodoxy. Elijah had a living relationship with God: *"O Lord, God of Abraham, Isaac, and Israel, let it be known this day that you are God in Israel, and that I am your servant, and that I have done all these things at your word. Answer me, O Lord, answer me, that this people may know that you, O Lord, are God, and that you have turned their hearts back"* (1 Kings 18:36-37). God's Spirit controlled his life, even when it meant exposing himself to risk and destruction (1 Kings 18:12, 46; 2 Kings 2:16). His God was not abstract or intellectual. He was more real to Elijah than anything perceived with the senses. Like Abraham, Elijah's life was stamped by a felt communion with God.

We see the same thing in the New Testament. The disciples engaged *with one accord* in prayer (Acts 1:14). We see that Paul rebuked the Galatians for thinking they could continue in the Christian life without the Holy Spirit: *Are you so foolish? Having begun by the Spirit, are you now being perfected by the flesh?* (Galatians 3:3). In another place, Paul proclaims, *The Spirit himself bears witness with our spirit that we are children of God* (Romans 8:16). He told the Ephesians to *be filled with the Spirit* (Ephesians 5:18). John says, *The anointing that you received from him abides in you.* He continued, *His anointing teaches you about everything, and is true, and is no lie* (1 John 2:27).

When it pertains to the Christian life, the language of the New Testament is overtly experiential. How could it be otherwise? The Holy Spirit does not stop His work in the Christian when He regenerates him. He is alive in us. He communes with us, encourages us, strengthens us, and revives us. This is why the Bible is filled with expressions of emotion: joy, sorrow, hope, fear, peace, love, and gratitude are just a few examples that come to mind. The fruit of the Spirit is love, joy, and peace (Galatians 5:22). Christ Himself is a man of sorrow, love, joy, anger, anguish, and peace. The apostle John is called the *Apostle of Love* because of his regular emphasis on that emotion. In fact, Scripture routinely condemns a lack of godly emotion as *hardness of heart* (Mark 3:5; Mark 16:14).

We must keep religious experience in biblical perspective, but the idea of experience cannot be tossed out without serious ramifications to the Christian life, which is what we see with dead orthodoxy. We are dealing here with a felt Christ. A living God. Unction. Power. Outpourings of the Spirit. The Scriptures and the testimony of church history show us that genuine Christianity is largely a matter of the experiential. Not every emotion or experience is legitimate, but to have no emotion or experience is just as problematic. Yes, we all have different temperaments, characters, backgrounds, and degrees of sanctification that will ensure our range or sensitivity to such things will never be monolithic. Yet if we are in Christ, we have the Holy Spirit indwelling us, which is bound to produce effects. When this is not the case, it is imperative to ask whether or even why our orthodoxy appears dead.

To frame it another way, if our doctrine of the Holy Spirit has no room in it for mighty outpourings of God or for the unusual and experiential, is it really the Holy Spirit we see in the Bible? If we scoff at the idea of experiencing God or of our devotion to God leading to subjective experiences such as awe, love, joy, and humility, we are not being honest about what the Scriptures present as a normal reality of the Christian life. This is the thrust of the chapters that follow.

THE DEADLINESS OF DEAD ORTHODOXY

I am convinced dead orthodoxy is more dangerous than the excesses we see in charismatic circles. This is not because the excesses in the charismatic world are innocent. They are not. But the excesses of charismania are obvious. They are absurd and attract attention. They make you run. They make your hair crawl. Dead orthodoxy is harder to detect. It is stale, arid, stuffy, and safe. More than anything else, it is safe and hence too dull to gain notice until it has already evaporated any spiritual vigor that was there. Our excessive fears of charismania and other legitimate problems in the Christian world have swung many of us into the realm of stiffness and cold, where we are suspicious of any emotion, experience, or warmth. The effects of this have been costly.

But there are other expressions of dead orthodoxy that are just as prevalent in our culture today. It can also take the form of easy believism, where a person culturally identifies as a Christian, wears a cross necklace, goes to church now and then, says a prayer before meals, and feels very secure that he is right with God even when there is an absence of real belief. It is merely going through the motions. While the staid and dry form of dead orthodoxy is more common in the northern and midwestern parts of the country, this other type of dead orthodoxy is rampant in the Bible Belt of the United States.

Thus, wherever we live and whatever church tradition we are in, we need orthodoxy to become warm again. But for this to happen, we must first determine why orthodoxy became so dead in the first place. What has gone wrong and how can we fix it? Do we ever pause to wonder why the church in the West seems so weak and powerless today and why we ourselves often feel this way? Why does our faith never seem to shake the world? Why do the glory days of the Reformation and Great Awakenings seem like mere fantasies and pixie dust compared to what our eyes behold today? Is it because our orthodoxy is dead? Is it because we have the wood and matches of religion but no fire from the Holy Spirit?

Dealing with such a topic as dead orthodoxy is bound to cut and wound. Thus, I have tried to conclude each chapter with a call to look to Jesus, *the founder and perfecter of our faith* (Hebrews 12:2). I have also tried to approach this subject with an amicable and gracious tone, even if there are necessary chidings along the way. There is dead orthodoxy in us all, but there is also hope found outside of ourselves. We serve an almighty God. Thus, we can be hopeful that the deadness that prevails both in the church and, all too often, in our own hearts can be thawed. Only Jesus can rescue us from such a peril, and for those who know Him, He already has. As we pick our way through the boneyard of dead orthodoxy, it is imperative we keep turning back to Christ, who is the perfect example of what it looks like when right affection, right practice, and right orthodoxy are all fused together.

STUDY QUESTIONS

1. What are some ways dead orthodoxy can manifest itself? Provide specific examples.

2. Do you think the phrase *dead orthodoxy* is appropriate, or is there another word or phrase to better describe the issue at hand?

3. What is your opinion of Blaise Pascal's description of his conversion (see above)? What are some pros and cons of such an experience?

4. How and where does dead orthodoxy show up in your own life?

CHAPTER 2

ARE YOU BORN AGAIN?

Are you born again? The phrase is familiar enough to anyone who is a Christian. It is also a phrase that has been cheapened by repetition. This was not always the case, however.

At the time of the Great Awakening in the 1740s, it was a scandalous question. Dead orthodoxy filled the pulpits, and the church had grown cold. Formalism, a problem we will address, reigned supreme. People knew the teachings of the Bible. They had been baptized. They were good church people. Many were sons and daughters of the Puritans. But a hardness had settled in. The vigor of the previous century had ossified. Christianity had become a playground for rationalism, deism, and unitarianism. It was without life or heart, and true spirituality appeared to have vanished.

Although there were exceptions, this was the general state of things when George Whitefield began to preach "You must be born again." His journals tell us that many professing Christians rejected the message.[3] One offended woman came up to him

---

3   E.g., see Whitefield's diary entries for December 24, 1738, and January 8, 1739.

and barked, "Mr. Whitefield, why do you keep saying to us you must be born again?" Whitefield replied, "Because, dear woman, you must be born again."

The idea of being born again was strange to these Christian people. It was offensive. You simply did not talk that way to good, moral folks who went to church every Sunday. Wasn't that proof enough of this *new birth*?

DEAD ORTHODOXY: WHERE TO BEGIN?

Dead orthodoxy is common enough in Christian circles today, but deciding which thread to pull at in the hope of unraveling the problem is complicated. As with any disease, the symptoms of dead orthodoxy manifest themselves in all kinds of ways. This could include a proud smugness, a disdain for revival, or a fear of anything out of the ordinary. But these things are merely the symptoms. What is the root issue? What is the cause of the symptoms? What is the disease itself?

This is why we first must examine the heart of the person who is exhibiting signs of dead orthodoxy. We need to do this judiciously because all Christians are prone to show some signs of dead orthodoxy, as mentioned in the previous chapter. Symptoms of dead orthodoxy do not always mean an unregenerate heart, yet they often do. A person can have correct theology and still be dead in their sins.

Jesus discussed this fact with Nicodemus. He told him, "*Truly, truly, I say to you, unless one is born again he cannot see the kingdom of God*" (John 3:3). The word Jesus used for *see* means something more than visual perception. He was talking about a certain kind of knowledge. It is not just a head knowledge, however. He was speaking here of the knowledge Adam had of his wife, Eve. It is more than intellectual awareness. It is that, but it is more than that. It is intimate. It is transformative. It is a kind of enlightenment or illumination, a eureka moment. Jesus told Nicodemus that unless a man is born again, he cannot even comprehend the true nature of the kingdom of God. He will be blind to it. He can hold to some axioms or principles about it, but he cannot go beyond that. This man will not be able to appreciate or understand the affection that such a kingdom should produce. There will be no warmth or love for such a kingdom. It will be as dry as calculating a math problem in a class you do not really like. Sure, you can figure out the answer, but you never get to the essence of it. You never take delight in it.

More to the point, a strictly intellectual apprehension of the gospel does not bring about conversion nor does it produce the harvest of the Holy Spirit: love, joy, peace, patience, kindness, goodness, faithfulness, gentleness, and self-control. Correct doctrine alone does not cause a person to be born again. If that is all there is, Christianity is merely a philosophy. It is intellectualism. This was the prevailing spiritual state in the 1700s before the Great Awakening, and it is the state of things in many corners of the church today. Get baptized. Learn your catechism. Say a prayer. Try to live a pious life. But any talk of the Holy Spirit producing in a person a change, a warmth, an experience, a tenderness, or even a deadness to the world and its pomp is unacceptable language to many in the Christian church, including those we would consider to be orthodox in doctrine.

OBJECTIVE VS. SUBJECTIVE

Here is another way to put it. Doctrine deals with the objective side of the faith. It is a necessary component to the faith, but it is not the whole story. The phrase *being born again* involves far more than just the objective aspects. It deals equally with the subjective, the experiential. This is why Christianity, of necessity, leads to an emphasis on the action and the activity of the Holy Spirit working in a person, a church, a denomination, or all the above. The Holy Spirit's work changes a person. It transforms him and makes him alive. He becomes something entirely new. What man does or grasps intellectually accomplishes nothing if it is not attended by the power of God. Merely laying hold of right doctrine does not effect the new birth. It does not change a person's heart.

This is why real Christianity inevitably must lead to *experiences*, and why *experience* should not be dismissed or downplayed as it so often is, especially in Christian circles that emphasize doctrine. No doubt, there can be excessive and even dubious kinds of experience, but it does not mean we should dismiss experience altogether. We must not let the unbiblical extremes out there tarnish our awe of the supernatural. Experience and right theology go hand in hand. The Reformers and Puritans used to speak in the language of *visitations of the Spirit, experimental* or *experiential religion, withdrawings, strengthenings,* and so on. They were sensitive to this subjective side of things. They understood that being born again implies something more than merely the objective or doctrinal, as important as that element is.

Scripture illustrates this. When Jesus was walking on the road to Emmaus with the two disciples Cleopas and Simon, He talked with them about Himself out of the Old Testament. Their hearts were burning within them, but it is not until they were at table with Jesus that we are told *their eyes were opened* (Luke 24:31). This does not mean they were physically blind up until that point, but rather that spiritually, experientially, subjectively, they had been. What is their first reaction to this new insight? Action. Movement. Transformation. *And they rose that same hour and returned to Jerusalem,* which was seven miles away on foot (Luke 24:33). The journey would have been dark and perilous. When they arrived in Jerusalem, they burst into the room where the disciples were staying and exclaimed what would become one of the most popular slogans of faith in the early church: *"The Lord has risen indeed!"* (Luke 24:34). Before God opened their eyes, they were *looking sad* (Luke 24:17). They were trudging along. They were anything but lively or animated. Why were they in this state? Because *their eyes were kept from recognizing him* (Luke 24:16).

This is why Reformed churches have a *Prayer of Illumination* in their services, typically before the sermon. It is a recognition that the Holy Spirit must open our eyes if we are to understand the Scriptures properly. We can hear the Scriptures read. We can read them for ourselves. We can hear the Word of God preached. We can grasp propositional truth claims and can assent to their veracity. But the subjective component to the faith cannot be ignored, and whenever it is ignored, the result is dead orthodoxy. Thus, there must be an awakening that takes place within us. Our eyes must be opened. This awakening can only come from outside us, which is why the Bible describes the Holy Spirit as something like the wind, blowing wherever He wishes but utterly necessary if there is to be a rustling or stirring within the trees, which here is a reference to the soul of the person. This is what it is to be born again or born from above. *"The wind blows where it wishes, and you hear its sound, but you do not know where it comes from or where it goes. So it is with everyone who is born of the Spirit"* (John 3:8).

MORE EXAMPLES FROM HISTORY

Jesus's miracles, especially the healing of the blind, point to this same reality. Matthew describes a scene where a group of blind men cried out to Jesus, *"Lord, let our eyes be opened." And Jesus in pity touched their eyes, and immediately they recovered their sight and followed him"* (Matthew 20:33-34). These men were physically blind. Jesus opened their eyes differently than the way He opened the eyes of Cleopas and Simon at the supper table. But the healing of the blind has spiritual significance. In one sense, we could describe these healings as parables. They point to a transcendent reality. They point to the illumination or the awakening of the blind soul by the hand of the Holy Spirit.

Mark provides an even better illustration. He recorded only two healings of blind men, but one comes directly after a scene where Jesus described the disciples as blind in this spiritual sense: *"Do you not yet perceive or understand? Are your hearts hardened? Having eyes do you not see?"* (Mark 8:17-18). Four verses later, Jesus healed a blind man at Bethsaida. Jesus shows His disciples what must happen to them spiritually. The eyes of their hearts must be healed. The eyes of their souls must be opened.

In John's Gospel, Jesus healed a man born blind. Then, because the blind man would not denounce Jesus, the man was kicked out of the synagogue. Jesus comforted the man by saying, *"For judgment I came into this world, that those who do not see may see, and those who see may become blind"* (John 9:39). The Pharisees overheard this statement and tried to grasp His meaning. They asked Jesus point blank if He thought they were blind as well. This can only be a reference to their spiritual condition since none of them were physically blind. Jesus said, *"If you were blind, you would have no guilt; but now that you say, 'We see,' your guilt remains"* (John 9:41). Had they recognized themselves as spiritually blind, they would have sought the Lord and had their spiritual eyes opened. But because they did not see themselves as spiritually blind, they remained spiritually blind. The church at Laodicea is charged with the same thing in Revelation: *"Anoint your eyes with eye salve, that you may see"* (Revelation 3:18 NKJV).

We can find this idea of experiential illumination even in ancient literature. Plato's *Allegory of the Cave* has long been seen as an example of the Christian concept of the new birth. I am not suggesting Plato was a Christian or even a Christian prophet as some in church history have maintained. But it is clear that some of his analogies and insights, this one especially, are striking examples of the idea we are discussing. Plato has us imagine a scene where there are prisoners in a cave, chained against a wall, looking out onto another wall where they see shadows. Above and behind them is a fire. Around the fire are workers. The prisoners never see the fire or the men because they are chained to the wall looking straight ahead. They have been chained to the wall as long as they can remember. The shadows on the wall are all they know of reality. Even the sounds they hear are merely echoes bouncing off the wall and into the ear. But then one of the prisoners breaks free:

> When one was freed from his fetters and com-
> pelled to stand up suddenly and turn his head
> around and walk and to lift up his eyes to the light,
> and in doing all this felt pain and, because of the
> dazzle and glitter of the light, was unable to dis-
> cern the objects whose shadows he formerly saw,
> *what do you suppose would be his answer if some-*
> *one told him that what he had seen before was all a*
> *cheat and an illusion, but that now, being nearer to*
> *reality and turned toward more real things, he saw*
> *more truly?* (italics mine)[4]

The prisoner then leaves the cave, where he is "blinded by the light." Eventually his eyes habituate. He sees the stars, the moon, trees, birds, and blades of grass. He is overwhelmed by this new insight. He realizes all he had known before was an illusion made of shadows and echoes. The man begins to pity his friends who are still chained to the cave, so like a good Christian, he goes back and tells them that although they are

---

4   Plato, *The Collected Dialogues*, ed. Edith Hamilton and Huntington Cairns, trans. Paul Shorey (Princeton, NJ: Random House, 1963).

blind, he can help direct them to the truth of things. He can point them to the real light. But his friends laugh at him and mock him. They would even kill him for trying to untie their bands: "And if it were possible to lay hands on him and to kill the man who tried to release them and lead them up, would they not kill him?"[5] Plato's analogy, while not perfect, is suggestive of exactly the theme with which we have been wrestling: the need to be *reborn* or illuminated from above.

The Scriptures also give us this idea when using the word *light*. David said, *The LORD is my light and my salvation* (Psalm 27:1). Jesus said about Himself, *"I am the light of the world"* (John 8:12). But we are told in the beginning of John's Gospel that the darkness did not *comprehend* Him or *grasp* Him, depending on the translation (John 1:5). The idea of comprehension in this sense is the same idea mentioned in Jesus's conversation with Nicodemus. It is a supernatural awareness. It is a knowledge that transcends mere intellectual belief or even assent. It is a type of subjective revelation given by God to the individual for the sake of believing and trusting in the truth of the gospel. It is God grasping hold of the believer in such a way that the person becomes *a new creation*, a new person. It is an act of God by which He gives spiritual life to a person, resulting in the whole of their existence being funneled in a godward direction. It is the freed prisoner emerging from the cave to see the truth. It is the idea found in Charles Wesley's hymn, "And Can It Be":

Long my imprisoned spirit lay
Fast bound in sin and nature's night;
Thine eye diffused a quick'ning ray,
I woke, the dungeon flamed with light;
My chains fell off, my heart was free;
I rose, went forth and followed Thee.

---

5   Plato, *The Collected Dialogues.*

Another metaphor we find in the Scriptures to explain this idea of the new birth is being *awakened*. Solomon spoke of natural sleep: *He gives to his beloved sleep* (Psalm 127:2). We see that Christ slept in the boat (Matthew 8:24), and the disciples slept when they should have been praying (Matthew 26:40). This is natural sleep. But there is also spiritual sleep. It is akin to deadness, but not necessarily the same thing. Genuine Christians can be asleep at times, and when they are, they need to be awakened. Paul told the Christians in Corinth to *awake to righteousness* (1 Corinthians 15:34 NKJV). Paul told some in the Ephesian church, *"Awake, O sleeper, and arise from the dead, and Christ will shine on you"* (Ephesians 5:14). Notice Paul wrote this letter to a church, but he realized certain people there needed to be roused. They needed to be awakened. This is the idea of the alarm clock ripping into what are otherwise peaceful dreams. The sound forces us awake. It startles, even annoys us, which is often the case when we first begin to see the truth of our lost state.

Many professing Christians are asleep today. This is one of the major reasons for dead orthodoxy. Some people merely go through the motions of Christian activity. For them, church is a doldrum. Prayer is a chore. Sharing the gospel with the neighbors is not even a consideration. They need to be awakened from their sleep. They need the same reminder Paul gave the Romans: *The hour has come for you to wake from sleep* (Romans 13:11).

WHO IS JESUS TO YOU?

Who Jesus is to you is the first thing you need to investigate when dealing with the problem of dead orthodoxy. Is the deadness a result of a dead soul? Is your soul spiritually moribund or blind? Do you have an intellectual relish for theology, polemics, debate, even the Scriptures, but find no change taking place as a result?

Such a phenomenon is seen in universities across the West. You can find classes on Christianity in every university, including the secular ones, but they are typically taught by scholars who do not have any affection for Jesus. These professors have a passion for studying the Gospels. They could not have made it through the grind of doctoral research without at least a spark of interest in such things. Similarly, most of the students in these classes find the topic to be interesting. They believe Jesus was an intriguing figure. They think the whole idea of people following this man so zealously, even to the point of death, is outrageous but fascinating. Some know the church's creeds and confessions backward and forward. They could teach the creeds in two or three different languages if they had to. But it is simply an intellectual interest. It is a hobby. They consider the Bible a good work of literature, something to debate, discuss, and dissect, but not be changed by or be too fanatical about. They master, systemize, and recite the Bible without ever coming to personal repentance toward God and faith in our Lord Jesus Christ.

Is this you? Has God worked in your heart so that you are no longer apathetic, cold, and dead to the things of God? Have you been born again? Are you now in a place where you love Him, delight in Him, and long to spend time with Him? Who is Jesus to you? Is He your Rock? Is He your Advocate? Is He your faithful High Priest and the Shepherd of your soul? Is He your Rose of Sharon and your Lily of the Valley? The one who is closer than a brother? Is He the pearl worth more than all the other pearls in the world? The gold in the field so precious that you would part with everything you have to possess it?

We saw at the beginning of the chapter that Whitefield was a preacher of the new birth. But that is because he himself was the dramatic recipient of such a miracle. After reading Henry Scougal's book *The Life of God in the Soul of Man* (1677),

Whitefield saw "that I must be born again or be damned." He cried out to the Lord, "If I am not a Christian, if I am not a real one, for Jesus Christ's sake, show me what Christianity is, that I may not be damned at last." Whitefield came to discover that true religion "is a vital union with the Son of God, Christ formed in the heart," whereupon "a ray of divine life did then break in on my poor soul."[6] Has this ray of divine life broken in on your soul? Has Christ shown you what real, living, experiential Christianity is?

If not, we have already found our problem. Ask the Lord to take out your stony heart and give you a heart of flesh, one alive and sensitive to the things of God, sin, and your neighbor (Ezekiel 36:26). The Lord is the one who gives sight to the blind. He is the friend of sinners. He is the one who came to seek and to save those who are lost. Go to Him today. Call on Him now. Do not wait. Jesus says, *"If you then, who are evil, know how to give good gifts to your children, how much more will the heavenly Father give the Holy Spirit to those who ask him!"* (Luke 11:13).

For those who are born again, however, this is just the beginning. The situation is more complex. What is the relationship between orthodoxy and orthopraxy, and why is it that even Christians often exhibit areas of deadness? How can even sound churches become so sleepy? That will be the investigation of the rest of this book.

STUDY QUESTIONS

1. Do you think the question, "Have you been born again?" is an appropriate question to ask people, both Christians and non-Christians? Explain the phrase as simply as possible.

---

6   George Whitefield, *The Revived Puritan: The Spirituality of George Whitefield*, ed. Michael Haykin (Peterborough, Ontario: Joshua Press, 2000), 25–26.

2. Do you think Plato's *Allegory of the Cave* is a fitting analogy of Christian conversion? Why or why not?

3. Do you agree with the distinction made between objective and subjective sides of the faith? What is their relationship with each other? Can you have one without the other?

4. If someone you know has not been born again, what steps can you take to help?

CHAPTER 3

ASHAMED OF THE CROSS?

In 2017, my friend and I were eating in a restaurant in Albuquerque. At some point during the meal, my friend handed a gospel tract to the waitress. He was respectful about it. He exuded the love of Christ. But my first instinct was embarrassment. I was uncomfortable. But was my friend wrong to do this? Of course not. I was wrong for being embarrassed by my friend sharing the gospel with a stranger. I wanted her and the others around us to see me as sophisticated, proper, and respected. Compared to my friend's, my orthodoxy was dead. His was very alive. His belief in Jesus was more than just an academic exercise or something to appease his conscience in preparation for death. It was vigorous and bearing fruit. The world or even other Christians may have viewed the encounter as awkward or embarrassing, but my friend was preaching the gospel to a lost soul. He was ready in season and out of season (2 Timothy 4:2). I was silent. I was proper. I was respectable.

To dead orthodoxy, the most egregious thing in the world is to be considered a radical, an enthusiast, a fanatic, or a fundamentalist. The natural reaction then is to become overly proper, formal, academic, dignified, and intellectual. Another word for this would be *respectable*.

RESPECTABLE CHRISTIANITY

Respectable Christianity is the number one driver of dead orthodoxy. This does not account for all cases of dead orthodoxy, as we will see later, but most of them. This makes perfect sense. Who wants to be considered backward or bigoted? Who wants to be seen as a zealot in a society where intolerance is the greatest sin? Who wants to experience what Paul and his band of preachers did: *We are cursed, . . . we are persecuted, . . . we are slandered. . . . We have become the scum of the earth, the garbage of the world* (1 Corinthians 4:12-13)?

There is a scene in the classic movie *Sheffey* (1977) that illustrates this problem of respectable Christianity.[7] Sheffey had just been converted at a Methodist house meeting. This was the 1800s, so such things happened. He went to tell his wealthy Presbyterian aunt who had been concerned about his embarrassing, immoral behavior for quite some time. Sheffey assumed she would be ecstatic at the news of his conversion. After all, she was a Christian. She went to church. But his aunt was livid, telling him that his enthusiasm over the whole thing was reckless and improper. Christianity for her was about respectability. It was about living a moral life. It was about staying out of trouble and not rocking the social boat. It was dignified. It was prim. Eventually, she told him to leave her house for his refusal to part ways with his enthusiastic type of Christianity. It did not fit in with her tamer type.

Later in the movie, the aunt was converted and wrote a letter of apology to her nephew, telling him she was finally aware

---

7   *Sheffey*, directed by Katherine Stenholm (1977; Greenville, SC: Unusual Films, 2020), DVD.

of how superficial her Christianity had been. She had had a dead orthodoxy. She was part of a historic denomination, and she knew her catechism. She likely tithed big sums of money every week. But she did not know what it meant to count the cost of following Christ. She did not know that the cross was a reproach. For her, Christianity was not supposed to be foolish in the eyes of the world. It was not supposed to be lively or enthusiastic. In fact, the opposite was true. She was a moral and churchgoing woman, but she resented any practice that the world or nominal Christians around her could describe as fanatical. For her, this would be heinous.

HYPOCRISY IN THE EARLY CHURCH

But why is respectable Christianity a contradiction to real Christianity? Another way to put it is to ask why Christianity is so unattractive to the wise or wealthy of the world. Paul says as much in his first letter to the Corinthians. *For consider your calling, brothers: not many of you were wise according to worldly standards, not many were powerful, not many were of noble birth* (1 Corinthians 1:26). Even Jesus thanks the Father *"that you have hidden these things from the wise and understanding and revealed them to little children"* (Matthew 11:25).

But why is this the case? Why aren't many wise turning to Christ? Why not many powerful? Why not people of nobility? Why not the dignified or respectable? Why did Jesus say, *"It is easier for a camel to go through the eye of a needle than for a rich person to enter the kingdom of God"* (Mark 10:25)? The reason is simple. The cross, by its very design, is meant to be scandalous. It is shameful. It is a reproach. It is an emblem of scorn and ignominy.

For those living in the West today, this is hard to understand. We wear cross necklaces and get crosses tattooed on our necks.

There is no reproach in being identified with the actual emblem of the cross. This is the fruit of cultural Christianity. It has led to nominalism, which is another term for dead orthodoxy. In Paul's day, dead orthodoxy was not as big of a problem. Being a Christian meant being put to death or, at the very least, persecuted. You lost your house (Hebrews 10:34). You were stoned (Acts 7:59-60). If being a Christian means losing your life or temporal comforts, you do not become a Christian unless it really means something to you. You do not go to church. You do not spend time together with Christians. You certainly do not profess Jesus to others. The cost is too high. The description of the early church in Acts perfectly illustrates this truth: *None of the rest dared join them, but the people held them in high esteem* (Acts 5:13). Everyone watched what was going on from a distance, but they would not risk their necks to join them. They were impressed by the unmistakable mark of the supernatural on them, but that was as far as it went.

PETER'S DEAD ORTHODOXY

Yet, when dead orthodoxy does appear in the pages of Scripture, especially among Christians, we see how swiftly it is dealt with, even if it is found in a person such as Peter.

In Galatia, Peter had no problem eating and being among the Gentiles, that is, until the Jewish Christians from Jerusalem came on the scene. Then he retreated in shame. He refused to be around the Gentile Christians at all. But why did he retreat? Peter had seen the power of God fall on the Gentiles in the same way it fell on the Jewish Christians (Acts 10:44). Peter had received a vision approving of this very thing (Acts 10:9-22). The Gentile Christians were just as much Christians as the Jewish Christians. This is the same Peter who defended his going to the Gentiles and staying under their roof when questioned by James and the other apostles in Jerusalem: *If then God gave the same gift to them as he gave to us when we believed in the Lord Jesus Christ, who was I that I could stand in God's way?"* (Acts 11:17). Even more bizarre is that he had even received the blessing of the apostles for this action: *When they heard these things they fell silent. And they glorified God, saying, "Then to the Gentiles also God has granted repentance that leads to life"* (Acts 11:18).

So what happened in Galatia? How do we account for Peter's embarrassment of the Gentile believers whenever the Jewish Christians visited? There is one explanation. He had a respectable type of Christianity. I am not suggesting that Peter's faith was counterfeit. There were times when he showed himself confident in the Lord and was better able to handle the reproach of the gospel. But in this instance, he waffled. He became squeamish. On one level, this is understandable. Jerusalem Christians could be a tough crowd. This is why James told Paul to identify himself with four Jewish Christians who were under a ceremonial vow so that the Christians in Jerusalem would know that Paul was not opposed to the observance of the law, at least for Jewish Christians at that time (Acts 21:17-26). But the situation in Galatia is different. Paul opposed forcing circumcision on non-Jewish believers, regardless of the firestorm such a view would cause. Paul and Peter both knew the gospel is by grace alone, through faith alone, in Christ alone, whether you are a Gentile or a Jew.

This is why Paul called Peter out. Peter was not acting consistently with the gospel. If the blood of Jesus was poured out for Gentiles also, why be ashamed of Gentile Christians? What is worse, Peter was not ashamed of Gentile Christians until the Jewish Christians arrived. Then it became an embarrassment for Peter. He started acting funny. He was being hypocritical, or two-faced. This is what dead orthodoxy is. Peter's view of the gospel was not off, at least not theoretically. But practically, his view of the gospel was not manifesting itself in his actions. Dead orthodoxy can be cunning, even in the heart of a foundational apostle. If Peter could be ensnared by dead orthodoxy, how much more is this true of us? In one situation, we are bold as lions. In another, we cower and sell out our Lord.

The problem of respectable Christianity also existed in the Galatian church as a whole. Perhaps this is what influenced Peter to act the way he did. He read the room and assessed the situation. According to Paul, there was a specific reason the Galatian church insisted on the Gentile converts being circumcised. They wanted to appear more respectable in the eyes of the Jewish Christians. *It is those who want to make a good showing in the flesh who would force you to be circumcised, and only in order that they may not be persecuted for the cross of Christ* (Galatians 6:12). The Galatian church was fearful of backlash if they did not require Gentile converts to be circumcised. They would be criticized, so they began requiring circumcision.

Sheffey's aunt had the same mindset. She was a Christian in order *to make a good showing in the flesh*. It was about respect. It was about looking dignified in the eyes of her peers. To be too enthusiastic or fanatical about the faith would bring persecution, so she ordered Sheffey to stop. For Peter and the Galatian church, to not circumcise Gentile converts would bring persecution. It would be too radical. It would be too offensive. The Galatians desired a tame, dignified Christianity, so they went along with the flow even if it meant rejecting a major tenet of the gospel.

Have we ever done this? Have we ever been embarrassed to hang out with Christians who are different, whose zeal is a little too over the top, a little too excessive? Or maybe we avoid Christians who do not know very much, those we consider more immature. Perhaps we do spend time with them but then speak condescendingly about them whenever we are around our own tribe again. Do we make the same kind of unbiblical discrimination that Peter made because of how people might view us? For instance, if I read a book by Leonard Ravenhill, will I secretly enjoy and learn from it but then scorn and critique it when I am around fellow Calvinists?[8] Will I suddenly be ashamed to say that there are truths to be found in it? What about a sermon by Adrian Rogers or an essay by C. S. Lewis?[9] It can go the other way too, of course. Charismatics enjoy Francis Schaeffer and Southern Baptists read Jonathan Edwards and Charles Spurgeon. But do they freeze when they think their clan will ostracize them for doing so? The notion of tribalism is addressed later, but for now, consider this question: Have we become so respectable that we are ashamed to be around or learn from other Christians?

THE OFFENSE OF THE CROSS

In-house embarrassment is not the only form of respectable Christianity. The bigger issue is our embarrassment of Christ when we are around unbelievers. We try to neutralize the scandal of the cross. Today the cross is just a symbol, a logo. Christianity is just one of many religions. It is an institution. It is a club. In fact, it is not even that for most people in the West. It is flippantly described as a "relationship." It is something you do alone, and only when convenient.

But for Paul, the cross was much more than this. He told the church in Corinth, *We preach Christ crucified* (1 Corinthians 1:23). This is a dramatic statement. In some sense, it is an appalling one. The people in his day would have thought so, at least. You did not preach about crucifixion in the first century, especially if such a thing happened to the One you are proclaiming to

---

8   Leonard Ravenhill (1907–1994) was a British evangelist and author known for his calls for prayer, revival, and holy living.

9   Adrian Rogers (1931–2005), an American pastor and author, served as president of the Southern Baptist Convention.

be the Lord of the cosmos. Even as late as AD 200, a Christian named Alexamenos was ridiculed for "worshiping his god," who was illustrated as a crucified donkey. In the first three centuries, you simply did not worship someone who had been hung on a cross. You certainly did not preach about it. Why not? Because it was not respectable. It was embarrassing. It was the same perspective of many today regarding Christianity. We want Christianity to be respectable. We want it to be seen as intellectually refined. We want it to be attractive. But that is exactly the opposite of what Paul called for when writing to the Corinthian church. The cross is foolish. It is ugly. It is moronic. But therein lies its power and its bite.

In the first century, crucifixion was a practice especially reserved for a specific type of criminal. Not everyone was despicable enough to hang on a cross. It was for rebels. It was for those who rebelled against their masters and for those who rebelled against the state. It was meant to be savage and hideous. Josephus called it "the most wretched of deaths."[10] Varro the Grammarian said that even the sound of it, *crux*, was harsh on the ears.[11] If the one you worshiped died like that, you would not talk about it. You would try to hide it and cover that part up. It would be too disgraceful. More importantly, crucifixion demonstrated that God's hand was against the man, not for him.

This is why it would have been scandalous to follow Jesus in the early days of the church and explains why the disciples were hiding when Christ was put to death. The way of the cross is humiliation, not power. It is an announcement of profound weakness, not strength. It is foolishness to the world, not wisdom, which is why Paul's words are so odd. Why would he preach something that was interpreted in his own day as

---

10   Flavius Josephus, *War of the Jews*, in *The Genuine Works of Flavius Josephus, the Jewish Historian*, trans. Henry St. John Thackeray (Cambridge, MA: Harvard University Press, 1950), 7.203.

11   Tom Holland and Dominic Sandbrook, "Crucifixion," April 14, 2022, in *The Rest is History*, produced by Vasco Andrade, podcast, 01:07:00, podcasts.apple.com.

humiliation, weakness, defeat, and foolishness? This was what Nietzsche despised about Christianity more than anything else.[12] Christianity's success would reverse what were seen as the virtues in the classical world. In Paul's day, people considered beauty, strength, power, wealth, vigor, and prowess to be virtues. They valued conquering enemies with brawn, crushing the opposition, and self-glory – everything the cross was not. But Paul did not preach about beauty, strength, wealth, and prowess. He preached the cross. But because God moves on such a message through the Holy Spirit, it became obvious that the message was supernatural. It was otherworldly. The fact that within three centuries the Roman Empire would be overtaken by this strange message is one of history's most illuminating paradoxes.

THE CROSS AND THE WESTERN MAN

But why do Christians today seek to avoid being seen as foolish in the eyes of the world? Why do we quail at anything too enthusiastic when it comes to the Christian life? Why do we chafe at being called dumb or backward because of our faith? Is it because we are ashamed of the cross? The world looks to the powerful, the intellectual, the wise, the wealthy, and the attractive as its movers and shakers. If we follow Jesus, we will be disqualifying ourselves from this class of people. Like the Roman Empire of old, the virtues of our culture are beauty, strength, power, wealth, vigor, and prowess. We think we must embody such traits if we are to have any influence. We must be posh, intellectual, respectable, and sexy. But that is not the Pauline way. That is certainly not the way of the cross.

But the way of the cross is more than being a Christian in name. There is no problem with being a Christian in our culture,

---

12   Friedrich Nietzsche (1844–1900) was a German scholar most known for his criticism of Western morality and religion.

so long as it is a certain type of Christian. Pop stars and athletes can say they believe in Jesus without any pushback. Country artists can sprinkle the name *Jesus* into their lyrics and even be applauded for it. Television shows about Jesus can be green-lighted. Commercials about Jesus can be aired during the Super Bowl. The same is true of politicians and their speeches. They can say they are Christians and even put Christian maxims into their campaign slogans. There is no offense in this kind of thing, and it is a blessing that we have these freedoms. But if the pop star takes a stand for the unborn or expresses disapproval of LGBTQ groups based on his or her reading of the Scriptures, then there will be problems. The pop star will be canceled. He or she will lose fans. There will be death threats. If the athlete does the same thing, he could be cut from the team. If a politician takes seriously what the Scriptures say and tries to govern accordingly, he will be targeted as a radical and a madman. This is true even for the conservative politicians inside their own "conservative" party. The television show or commercial that accurately portrays the Jesus of the Bible would never be approved. If you get too serious about this Christian stuff, it becomes scandalous, and it is not allowed.

What is worse, nominal Christians will be just as likely to attack such vigorous expressions of the faith as the lost. They look on such things as embarrassing fanaticism or cultism. Respectable Christianity means we do not get too serious about our faith outside of church, and we criticize or ridicule any Christian who does. We distance ourselves from them. We make sure others know we are not "that type" of Christian. In other words, we do the opposite of what Paul did. He proclaimed the cross even though it was offensive. You could even say he proclaimed the cross *because* it was offensive. He was not try-ing to offend for the sake of being offensive, but he knew that because his culture considered the cross such a detestable and grotesque thing, to see people saved by it would prove it was the power of God. Nothing else could explain it.

The birth and ministry of Jesus reveal the same thing. Who expected the Savior to come out of Nazareth, a backwoods village without any influence? He was uneducated. He was a carpenter. He was Jewish. These three things would be repugnant to any Gentile. Also, this man was hung on a cross, which would be revolting to a Jew. Thus, whether you looked at Him as a Jew or as a Gentile, you would be scandalized by such a person. You would not follow Him and especially never offer Him worship. It is almost as if God determined to make the whole thing as despicable and unrespectable as possible in the eyes of the world. Why does God do so? Because when a person is converted, when a church is planted, when missionaries leave everything to go overseas, or when someone dies for the gospel or even takes a stand for the gospel in a culture such as ours, only the supernatural power of God can account for it. Thus, God alone gets all the glory.

This is why the gospel is *the wisdom of God*. Through an instrument of death, death is destroyed. Through the cross, we are healed. Rome's power symbol is transformed into a picture of humility, meekness, sacrifice, and suffering. It is a symbol of Christ overthrowing death, sin, darkness, hell, demons, and all earthly opposition. It is a declaration that God is in charge and that He has brought to naught the powers of this world. Charles Hodge said that the cross "has already changed the state of the intelligent universe, and it is to be the central point of influence throughout eternity."[13] But the scandalous nature of the cross demonstrates God's wisdom and power. Thus, if the cross loses its identity as foolish or as an image of reproach, what is left? Respectable Christianity. Dead orthodoxy.

---

13   Charles Hodge, *A Commentary on 1 & 2 Corinthians* (Carlisle, PA: Banner of Truth, 1974), 211.

THE CONVERSIONS OF THE WISE AND POWERFUL

It is not the norm, nor is the church dependent on it, but we cannot deny the fact that the Holy Spirit converts influential and powerful people. How do we explain this? At the time of his conversion, the apostle Paul was an influential Pharisee. Before their conversions, Augustine was a man of reputation, Justin Martyr was a philosopher, and Constantine the Great was an emperor. There was a tidal wave of kings converted to the faith in the Middle Ages, including Clovis and Charlemagne. Closer to our own time, giants like the athlete C. T. Studd and authors such as C. S. Lewis and T. S. Eliot all had notable influence prior to their conversions. Leo Tolstoy, who later felt sorry for those "empty" enough to have the need to read *Anna Karenina*, had already written two of the greatest books of all time before his conversion. If the typical way of conversion and advancement of God's kingdom is through the mean and lowly, what do we make of the rich, intelligent, and famous who do come into the kingdom, and what can it show us about the difference between a dead faith and a living one?

Paul the Apostle gave us a clue. After his conversion, he said he was the least of all the apostles and the chief of sinners (1 Corinthians 15:9; 1 Timothy 1:15). He saw no need to boast except in the cross of Christ. Augustine showed us the same thing. After his conversion, the successful orator longed to retreat into the darkness of obscurity for the purpose of better knowing God. T. S. Eliot suffered reproach from his friends, including Virginia Woolf, who worried the poet had gone mad because he turned to prayer and the Bible. These men were humbled. They were brought low, despite their obvious gifts. They knew God did not need them. His kingdom was not going to be better off now that they were on His side. They knew that if they were arrogant and boastful, they would be a hindrance to God's work on earth, not a help. The cliché often uttered among Christians in this case proves true: "Lord, don't let me get in the way." Paul and Augustine were aware of this, and so the Lord could use them. They seemed to genuinely consider themselves least out of all the saints. They knew they were replaceable.

This is why John Calvin said, "The mighty gifts with which we are endowed are hardly from ourselves; indeed, our very being is nothing but subsistence in the one God."[14] When a person knows this truth and genuinely believes it, they cannot help but be humbled. In fact, the more gifted a person is, the more he will be humbled, and that is why he turns to God. Calvin continued: "Thus, from the feeling of our own ignorance, vanity, poverty, infirmity, and – what is more – depravity and corruption, we recognize that the true light of wisdom, sound virtue, full abundance of every good, and purity of righteousness rest in the Lord alone. To this extent we are prompted by our own ills to contemplate the good things of God. We cannot seriously aspire to Him before we begin to become displeased with ourselves,"[15] which is something like being brought low before God. This was David's thought after God told him of the blessings that were to come through his seed: *Then King David went in and sat before the LORD and said, "Who am I, O Lord GOD, and what is my house, that you have brought me thus far?"* (2 Samuel 7:18). Even though he was a king, David was bewildered. He could not understand. This is what happens to the noble and mighty when they are converted.

Every genuine Christian, to some degree, is aware that any gifts or abilities we have are from God. This is part of the insight or wisdom that God works in the Christian at conversion. Without this mindset, they would have never turned to Christ in the first place. It is the very fact that these influential persons recognized the futility of being wise, noble, and powerful in

---

14   John Calvin, *Institutes of the Christian Religion*, ed. John T. McNeill (Philadelphia: Westminster Press, 1960), 1.1.1.

15   Calvin, *Institutes*, 1.1.1.

the eyes of the world, especially in contrast to the riches found in Christ, that set them apart from the world's ordinary type of wise, noble, and powerful.

But does the church today think this way? Men and women are attempting to be demigods on social media, in politics, in our houses and churches. The people of the world will worship themselves as supermen and women while downplaying their own moral filth. Accordingly, the Scriptures do not hold back when it comes to the woeful state of man. *"None is righteous, no, not one"* (Romans 3:10). *"No one seeks for God"* (Romans 3:11). *The LORD saw that the wickedness of man was great in the earth, and that every intention of the thoughts of his heart was only evil continually* (Genesis 6:5). *"The intention of man's heart is evil from his youth"* (Genesis 8:21). *In sin did my mother conceive me* (Psalm 51:5). This is why Christ says, *"Everyone who does wicked things hates the light and does not come to the light, lest his works should be exposed"* (John 3:20).

For the Christian, there is no room for any ambition to be respectable or dignified in the eyes of the world. Whether you are Augustine of Hippo or a Christian plumber in the backwoods of Texas, there is no difference between the two when it comes to the gospel. Both, if they are to be saved, come to realize the troubling darkness in their hearts and call out for Christ to cleanse them. Both receive grace and wisdom from God. Both use their respective vocations to the glory of God.

Whether you are wise and influential in the world's eyes is irrelevant to God. This is what Augustine realized. It is what Paul the Apostle realized. It is why they hurled themselves on the mercy of the Lord. It is why they fled the rags of worldly dignity: *Indeed, I count everything as loss because of the surpassing worth of knowing Christ Jesus my Lord. For his sake I have suffered the loss of all things and count them as rubbish, in order that I may gain Christ* (Philippians 3:8).

THE DECEPTION OF RESPECTABLE CHRISTIANITY

What makes respectable Christianity dangerous is its subtlety. Respectable Christianity can be orthodox. It can be theologically accurate. It can have read all the right books and be up to date on all the latest theological debates in the Christian world. It can tithe and live a moral life. But it has no power. It has no punch. It has no vivacity. It is dead. And worse, whenever there is a whiff of spiritual power or vitality in its midst, even within an individual's own heart, it is quickly snuffed out for fear that it could become too outlandish or excited and hence lose respectability. Respectable Christianity does not want to offend. It does not want to look too fanatical. It does not want the ire of the masses. It does not want to be looked down on. It is respectable, after all.

The tragedy of respectable Christianity is just this. What some are most ashamed of when it comes to the Christian faith is exactly where the bite is. Although *the cross* itself, as an emblem, is not offensive to the world today, living out the cross certainly is. Evangelism, standing against injustice, standing for righteousness and biblical morality, pursuing a holy life – even if it means your kids not playing in soccer games on Sunday or going to the movie with explicit nude scenes on Friday – will be an aroma of death to our culture. Respectable Christianity will do the polite thing, however. It will not turn down the movie invitation or challenge the merit of youth sports on Sundays. It will not bring the gospel to the gay neighbor across the street. It will not stick out its neck if it means losing the world's respect. Christians who do take this risk should not be rude and offensive but be aware that our faith comes with a cost. The power of the cross is visible when the Christian life is lived out in public, and it is then that the offense happens and the scandal is made obvious. Dead orthodoxy protects itself against this, but that is because it is dead. It desires respectability. It desires the status quo. But this is not the mindset of Christ, whose life was one of continuous scandal, controversy, reproach – anything but dead orthodoxy.

Respectable Christianity is the mark of a dying church and is what we see in the West today. The church will not take difficult stances or stick its neck out if it means pushback or resentment from the world. As much as we long for cultural capital and advancement of the gospel in the public realm, too much respectability has often been the downfall of the church. When we get too comfortable, we dread the scorn of the cross. This is true personally and corporately. We decreasingly depend on the Holy Spirit. We become self-confident and self-reliant. We are popular and liked. Because of indwelling sin, all Christians are prone to want the world's acceptance. We wince at the thought of our peers or neighbors seeing us as backward. Have we compromised to avoid reproach? Have we been embarrassed by others' zeal for the cross?

As we continue our investigation of dead orthodoxy, let us seek God's help in rooting out this poison of respectability. Let us remember Jesus, *who for the joy that was set before him endured the cross, despising the shame, and is seated at the right hand of the throne of God* (Hebrews 12:2). Paul wrote that Christ, *who, though he was in the form of God, did not count equality with God a thing to be grasped, but emptied himself, by taking the form of a servant, being born in the likeness of men. And being found in human form, he humbled himself by becoming obedient to the point of death, even death on a cross* (Philippians 2:6-8).

Jesus knew nothing of worldly respectability. From the moment He opened His mouth in public, He was an offense and a scandal. Any credibility with the movers and shakers of the world was immediately lost. But rather than vacillate, He embraced the offense, and in doing so, overturned sin and death. He is our model. He is our prototype. He was never embarrassed by the cross. Are we?

STUDY QUESTIONS

1. Besides the movie *Sheffey*, what other examples from our culture depict respectable Christianity?

2. How would living in a country where Christians are persecuted affect respectable Christianity?

3. Are there any other examples of the rich and famous being converted to Christianity?

4. Think of a time in your own life when you have acted like Peter did in Galatia. When have you acted like Paul, who boldly reproached Peter for his hypocrisy?

CHAPTER 4

MR. FORMALIST

We have all heard it before. Maybe we have even said it. "Christianity is a relationship, not a religion."

But according to James 1:26-27, this is not exactly true. Yes, Christianity at its heart is being in right relationship with God through Jesus Christ. But Christianity is also a religion. It has its own system of beliefs, symbols, traditions, and sacred narratives that give explanation to life and the universe. It has its own way of worship, even if the details vary from church to church. This is not necessarily a bad thing. It is simply what a religion is.

Christianity also has certain *forms* unique to itself. *Form* is a word used to describe norms of religious practice. For instance, there is a liturgy in every church service, even if the church rejects the idea of using liturgies. How is this so? Because liturgy just means the format used in the worship service. It comes from the idea of *public service*. It is the order put down in a bulletin. Some services are more structured than others, but it is impossible not to have some form or format by which the service is conducted. Otherwise, you would have an amorphous blob of chaos from beginning to end.

Another example of form would be the layout of the biblical canon. The canon has an order. It has a set structure. This is a good thing because it ensures all of us can read and communicate from the same book with a minimum of unnecessary confusion. Another form is church government. We may debate which one is most appropriate or biblical, but every church has some form of government. The same is true of doctrine. Every Christian believes the Bible teaches certain truths, and these truths can be organized in a certain way or format. Thus, religion and form, although not currently in vogue in the broader evangelical world, are things we cannot get rid of, nor should we want to. They are not just helpful, they are necessary. God is a God of order, not disorder. Although formal religion does not save, it is not true that all forms and all talk of Christianity as a religion should be discarded.

But what happens when order, religion, and tradition go too far? What happens when there is order and tradition, even good tradition, but no spiritual warmth, life, or vitality? What happens when there is a form of godliness but no power? You get dead orthodoxy. Another word for this is *formalism*. Speaking about his own day, the Puritan Thomas Hall said: "Formalism, formalism, formalism is the great sin of this day, under which the whole country groans. There is more light than there was but less life; more profession but less holiness."[16] This lament speaks equally true of our own times.

THE FORMALIST IN BUNYAN'S *PILGRIM'S PROGRESS*

In John Bunyan's *Pilgrim's Progress*, we meet a man named *Formalist*.[17] Although Bunyan does not describe this man at

---

16   Thomas Hall, as quoted by J. C. Ryle, "Formal Religion – 2 Timothy 3:5," accessed December 23, 2024, https://www.monergism.com/formal-religion-2-timothy-35

17   John Bunyan, *The Pilgrim's Progress* (Project Gutenberg; 2021), https://www.gutenberg.org/files/131/131-h/131-h.htm.

much length in *Pilgrim's Progress*, he comments on formalists in other places: The formalist "is a man that has lost all but the shell of religion. He is hot, indeed, for his form; and no marvel, for that is his all to contend for. But his form being without the power and spirit of godliness, it will leave him in his sins; nay, he stands now in them in the sight of God and is one of the many that *will seek to enter and will not be able*" (Luke 13:24).[18]

Bunyan assumed this man is unregenerate, and there is reason enough to think so. Notice this man is not without some heat or fervency, but the object of his heat is merely forms, traditions, and rituals. He is passionate about the husk or scaffolding of religion, not the thing itself. If one has the correct forms, it is enough. If one's doctrine is correct, it is enough. If one's church attendance is consistent, he is good to go. Spurgeon said, "Formalists think, 'We do not mind being christened, confirmed, taking the sacrament, and going to church or chapel; but this repenting of sin, this believing, this clinging to Christ, this seeking after holiness – ah! It is too far about.' They cry, 'Peace, peace; when there is no peace.'"[19]

The formalist believes that a right form or show of religion merits favor in the eyes of God. He is deceived into thinking that God is impressed with the externals, even when there is no heart worship. The Old Testament prophets denounced this error. In Hosea, God tells the people, *For I desire steadfast love and not sacrifice, the knowledge of God rather than burnt offerings* (Hosea 6:6). The problem is even more pronounced in Isaiah 1:

What to me is the multitude of your sacrifices?
says the Lord;
I have had enough of burnt offerings of rams

---

18 John Bunyan, *The Straight Gate: The Great Difficulty of Going to Heaven* (London, 1676), 74.
19 Charles Spurgeon, *Pictures from Pilgrim's Progress* (London: Counted Faithful, 1903), 76.

and the fat of well-fed beasts;
I do not delight in the blood of bulls,
or of lambs, or of goats.
When you come to appear before me,
who has required of you
this trampling of my courts?
Bring no more vain offerings;
incense is an abomination to me.
New moon and Sabbath and the calling of convocations –
I cannot endure iniquity and solemn assembly.
Your new moons and your appointed feasts
my soul hates;
they have become a burden to me;
I am weary of bearing them.
When you spread out your hands,
I will hide my eyes from you;
even though you make many prayers,
I will not listen;
your hands are full of blood. (Isaiah 1:11-15)

Such language may seem severe, and it is. God was speaking to a very religious group of people. They regularly appeared before God and were diligent in their offerings. They were careful to observe the Sabbath, convocations, new moons, and feasts, all of which were common observances in the days of the Old Testament. But something had gone terribly wrong. They were doing the right things externally, but God was clearly outraged. Why? Their religion was just a shell. It was what Jesus called a whitewashed tomb. The outside looks ritzy, but inside is nothing but bones and cobwebs. There is no life. There is no desire for God. It is dead orthodoxy.

This is what the temple had become in the days of Christ. The temple in Jerusalem was one of the wonders of the world.

It took several decades to complete, even with, at one time, as many as eighty thousand men working on it day and night. It was a huge complex, as large as eight football fields laid together. Its exterior was made of marble and gold. The Middle Eastern sun exploded off its walls, causing it to glow like snow for miles around. The treasury was inside the temple and held what would be equivalent in our day to 2.2 billion dollars. It was magnificent. It was flashy. It was religious. Priests offered sacrifices around the clock. Josephus estimated that fifty thousand lambs were sacrificed during Passover week alone. Pilgrims regularly thronged to the temple, and priests, scribes, and religious teachers dotted its grounds at all hours of the day.

Once, when they were at the temple, Jesus's disciples marveled at how glorious its stones and structure were. Jesus's reaction was not what they expected: *"Do you see these great buildings? There will not be left here one stone upon another that will not be thrown down"* (Mark 13:2). In AD 70, this is exactly what happened. A Roman army burned the city and the temple to the ground. There would never again be a priesthood, sacrifices, or a temple. It was all gone. Jesus said it was the result of the people of this exceedingly religious institution rejecting their Messiah. They clearly had a form of godliness. They were very zealous about the law and its performance. They were exacting in their rituals. But it was not enough. It was dead. It was a shell. The sacrifices were meant to point to the Messiah, Jesus of Nazareth. The temple itself was meant to point to the Messiah. Even the priesthood was meant to point to the perpetual priesthood of the Son of God. But none of this was happening, so God brought it to an end.

What of our forms, traditions, and religion today? How often do people go through the motions in their Christian lives, including on Sundays? The forms, traditions, and practices of the Christian faith are not always bad in themselves, but if they are not stirring up our affections for Christ, they become not only bad but also damnable. This is why Hebrews tells us:

> *Consequently, when Christ came into the world, he said, "Sacrifices and offerings you have not desired, but a body have you prepared for me; in burnt offerings and sin offerings you have taken no pleasure. Then I said, 'Behold, I have come to do your will, O God, as it is written of me in the scroll of the book.' And by that will we have been sanctified through the offering of the body of Jesus Christ once for all* (Hebrews 10:5-7, 10).

Doctrine, form, religion, and even tradition can be useful. Regarding doctrine, it is even proper to contend for such things. Right worship and church government are crucial. These are non-negotiables for any church. Precision is important to God, so we would be amiss to throw it aside. But it is not everything. For the prophets, the Puritans, Bunyan, and Spurgeon, it was merely the shell. For example, in *Pilgrim's Progress*, the Formalist is a religious performer. Worst of all, he is deceived by his performance. He thinks there is merit to it. He can see his religious exercises and his zeal, but they are not the real thing. They are counterfeits of the real things. There is no inward life. The formalist's strict adherence to prescribed or external forms masks the deadness of his heart. J. C. Ryle described it this way: "When a man is a Christian in name only, and not in reality – in outward things only, and not in his inward feelings – in profession only, and not in practice – when his Christianity in short is a mere matter of form, or fashion or custom, without any influence on his heart or life – in such a case as this, the man has what I call a 'formal religion.'"[20]

---

20 J. C. Ryle, *Practical Religion* (Newberry, FL: Logos, 2022), 129.

MORE HELP FROM CHURCH HISTORY

The Scottish minister Alexander Whyte (1836–1931) can help us better understand the difference between a healthy use of form and *formalism* proper. First, according to Whyte, formalism is the result of proper instruction, which makes it even more complicated: "We all began our religious life by being formalists. And we were not altogether to blame for that. Our parents were first to blame for that and then our teachers and then our ministers. They made us say our psalm and our catechism to them, and if we only said our sacred lesson without stumbling, we were straightway rewarded with their highest praise."[21] This is not wrong. Every Christian should catechize their children. So, what is the problem?

For Whyte, it is when knowledge of the catechism is enough. It is mere memorization, nothing else. The same is true of going to church or attending a Bible study. Do we do so merely because we are told to? This is the trap Bunyan himself had fallen into before he was a Christian:

> Because I knew no better, I fell in very eagerly with the religion of the times: to wit, to go to church twice a day, and that, too, with the foremost. And there should I sing and say as others did. Withal, I was so overrun with the spirit of superstition that I adored, and that with great devotion, even all things, both the high place, priest, clerk, vestment, service, and what else belonged to the church: counting all things holy that were therein contained. But all this time I was not sensible of the danger and evil of sin. I was kept from considering that sin would damn me, religion soever I followed, unless I was found in Christ. Nay, I never thought of Christ, nor whether there was one or no.[22]

---

21 Alexander Whyte, *Bunyan Characters* (1893; Project Gutenberg, 2005), https://www.gutenberg.org/files/1885/1885-h/1885-h.htm.

22 John Bunyan, *Grace Abounding to the Chief of Sinners* (1905; Project Gutenberg, 2013), https://www.gutenberg.org/files/654/654-h/654-h.htm.

Bunyan described himself as a false professor of Christ. His religion was in name only. It was a type of ritualism. What about us? Do we go to church, know our Bible, catechize our children, know plenty of doctrine, fulfill our duties, but have had no inward heart change? Are there any of you whose affections for Christ are never stirred or whose Christianity is merely rote or ritualistic? Perhaps you are a Christian because it was the way you were raised, or it is what you think you must do to stay out of hell. But is there any warmth or relish in your heart for the things of Christ, including the study of Scripture, praying, fellowship with the saints, attending worship on the Lord's Day, or growing in godliness and piety?

All Christians experience drought and deadness in their lives from time to time. I am not referring to that. What I am speaking of is more deep-seated, more insidious. Is your motive for going to church or reading your Bible to know God better? Many professing Christians are experts in theology but are contentious and harsh. Many know their confessions and creeds but refuse to forgive their enemies or spend any time in prayer, other than the formal, ritualistic type. Many professing believers have correct doctrine but lack love for the brethren, expressed by a lack of patience with the more immature. Many are exact in their family worship but have never known what Paul meant when he said, *God's love has been poured into our hearts through the Holy Spirit, who has been given to us* (Romans 5:5). Many people engage themselves in religious activities but consider them drudgery. Many are dead formalists. Many are ritualists, those who have a religion of rites and ceremonies without sense or substance.

If any of this resonates with you, the first thing to do is turn back to Jesus. Confess and repent, knowing there is forgiveness found in Him. Ask the Lord to warm your heart in the things of Him. Ask God for a fresh outpouring of His Spirit on your chapped soul: *"Come now, let us reason together, says the* LORD: *though your sins are like scarlet, they shall be as white as snow; though they are red like crimson, they shall become like wool"* (Isaiah 1:18).

FORMALISM AND PREACHING

This brings us to the subject of preaching. In some sense, everything begins with preaching. Preaching must aim at the heart. Its channel is through the head, yes, but it must not get stuck there. Preaching must lead to action and change in the hearer. Thus, preaching must direct itself to the emotions. The Puritans called this *painful* preaching. It does not mean that preaching needs to be harsh or mean but that it convicts and cuts and ultimately points to Jesus. Richard Sibbes said, "To preach is to woo," which is the same idea.[23] Preaching is meant to touch the affections of man, not just his intellect.

We have probably all heard the phrase, "As goes the pulpit, so goes the nation." This is undoubtedly true. But when it comes to dead orthodoxy, we can narrow it to the following: Where the pulpit goes, the pew goes. Or as the pulpit goes, so goes the church. Dead orthodoxy among Christians can often be attributed to dry, intellectual preaching. When the pulpit is dry, stuffy, and academic, the pew becomes so as well. This is not a call for preachers to start screaming, sweating, stomping, and waving their arms in the pulpit. Not necessarily. Much of preaching, especially its delivery, is an expression of temperament and personality. This is not a call for anyone to change their personalities or act insincerely just because they are preaching a sermon.

However, we must admit there is a problem in many orthodox circles with the delivery of sermons. It seems much of our

---

23   Richard Sibbes, who lived from 1577 to 1635, was an Anglican pastor and author. His best-known work today is a book on salvation, *The Bruised Reed.* He befriended and mentored many other influential pastors.

preaching is mere academic lecturing. In its worst form, sermons are read like dull press releases. In its more tolerable expressions, the preaching is very orthodox. Sermons are typically well-structured and expository, with a few Greek and Hebrew words sprinkled in, along with a plethora of technical terms that most people in the church have never heard explained. But there is no unction, no anointing, no call for action. There is no authority, pleading, or crying over souls. There is no wooing. Those in the circles of dead orthodoxy would deem this too fanatical or extreme. In those circles, preaching has become the opposite of experiential, unless the experience is boredom. It comes across as a pile of well-polished bones. And if the pulpit is cold, is it any wonder that the church will be cold as well?

This is why it could be useful to read homiletic books outside of your own tradition, especially if you are a preacher in a highly intellectual denomination. There will be much you can agree with in such books and some things you cannot, but many things will convict any sincere reader to the core. You will find words that we have been trained to consider tacky or too sensational, such as *inspire* or *vision casting*. The authors of those books will argue that one of the aims of the sermon is to inspire the congregation or to cast a vision for them. Our first response is disgust. What do you mean, *inspire* the congregation? Doesn't the Holy Spirit do that? And shouldn't doctrinal information inspire them, regardless of how we present it?

Yes and no. Yes, because only the Spirit can convict and draw. But if that means delivery and approach is irrelevant, then no, because that is not the way God has wired people. We are more than just brains. That is where these homiletic books excel. For example, good ones teach that the sermon should include all the things taught in seminary, such as using illustrations and staying close to the text, but preaching should also focus on revealing what will happen when the believer applies the sermon in his life. Pastors should help the congregation imagine the fruit that will result when they apply and practice what was taught in the sermon. The sermon is then very practical and accessible and preached with the congregation in mind.

This is not what usually happens in more intellectual traditions. The sermons in these traditions focus on information – on theory and doctrine. Because we have seen the loud and fanatic type of preaching, we become analytical and stiff. We become disembodied heads. What happens to the congregation sitting under such preaching? They become analytical and stiff as well. They become puffed up with knowledge but have little heart religion. There is plenty to criticize about the sermons coming out of the less intellectual traditions, but we must admit that they are good at inspiring, casting vision, pleading, and keeping the congregation in mind – and doing so with a certain amount of warmth.

The sermons found in Scripture are an even better example of warm homiletics. Look at the fire of John the Baptist, the ardency of Peter, the earnestness of Elijah, the tears of Jesus and Jeremiah, and the passionate perseverance of Paul. These men are anything but cold and rigid preachers. The reality of the supernatural in these men prevented them from taking their subject matter stiffly or analytically. Their love for souls induced feeling and passion. Paul said as much in his second letter to the Corinthians: *Knowing the fear of the Lord, we persuade others* (2 Corinthians 5:11).

Too often, our sermons are a way to highlight our own theological acumen and training, rather than a call to persuade, plead, and cry for men to turn to the Lord or to grow in grace. We do not expect anything to happen in our sermons because we see them as merely a dispensing of Bible information into the heads of our hearers. Such information is not bad as far as it goes, but as we have seen, it is deficient if that is all there is.

Does the information lead to worship? Does it lead to action, affection, and transformation? Does it lead to conversions? Do we even expect such things to take place? As goes the pulpit, so goes the pew. A dead pulpit will lead to a dead congregation. Formal preaching will lead to formal Christians.

THE FORMALIST'S HOPE

In *Pilgrim's Progress*, what surprised Christian most about Formalist is not his disdain for the gospel in preference to custom and tradition but that he refused to accept Christian's counsel about his soul. Formalist told Christian to "look to himself." Do not trouble your head about me, he told him. Like the rest of us, the formalist does not like to be corrected. His doctrine is precise, and his church attendance impeccable. Who are you to tell him he does not have the real thing or that there has been no heart work done in him?

I am not encouraging us to call out every person who is not as warm or zealous as we think ourselves to be, but I do want to encourage us to examine our own hearts and to consider the counsel we have received. The same is true of churches. Both individuals and churches can get to a place where they think that correct doctrine, an order of worship regulated by the Scriptures, God-exalting music, and expository preaching is everything they need. But without the Spirit of God, this is only the husk.

Realizing they need more, many churches resort to pragmatism, pomp, and externals instead of praying to God for an outpouring of the Holy Spirit. But pragmatism and pomp are just additional layers of formalism. They are trappings, not the real thing. Many churches today look to pageantry, liturgy, pragmatism, and other forms of religion to liven up their congregations and fill the spiritual void in their worship. Others lean on traditions and rituals that have survived "for more than a thousand years," as Bunyan told us. This is not necessarily bad, but if that is all there is, it is worse than bad. It would be better to have a church that sings off tune from the heart than one that sings on tune for the sake of self-glory. The same is true of sermons or prayers or any other practice in the church.

Formalism is rampant in many parts of the church today. We must not stop pointing people to the gospel, even those who think they are safe and are walking the path of religion. Formalism is the belief that acting like a Christian can make me a Christian, but our works, no matter how great our zeal, devotion, precision, and correctness, can never save us. Augustus Toplady's *Rock of Ages* (1776) serves as a reminder of this very thing:

> Could my zeal no respite know,
>   could my tears forever flow,
> all for sin could not atone;
>   thou must save, and thou alone.

The person and work of Jesus is the only way we are made right with God. He is the only road that leads to life. In *Pilgrim's Progress*, before Formalist goes off to his destruction, Christian warns him: "You come in by yourselves, without his direction; and shall go out by yourselves, without his mercy." If you have not had a real heart change that comes from encountering the living God, cry out to God to ask Him to give you not only the form of godliness but also its power. *For neither circumcision counts for anything, nor uncircumcision, but a new creation* (Galatians 6:15).

STUDY QUESTIONS

1. Is it helpful to describe Christianity as a relationship, not a religion? Why or why not?

2. What are some pros and cons of describing Christianity as a religion?

3. In what areas have you succumbed to religious formalism?

4. Why do you think God takes formalism so seriously?

CHAPTER 5

EVANGELISM'S BLOT

An excessive desire for respectability and its twin, Mr. Formality, lead to our next symptom of dead orthodoxy: an apathy for evangelism. This makes perfect sense. A person or church with a dead orthodoxy is very nice and moral but has no concern for the lost, no interest in the demise of the world.

Sure, dead orthodoxy frowns at the bestiality of the culture. It has a disdain for foul language, nudity, and sexual sins. It detests the ugliness it sees in the streets. But it has no desire to do anything about it. It has no pain in its heart for people ensnared in such wickedness. Dead orthodoxy mocks and criticizes the neighbors with the rainbow flag but never tells them about Jesus. Dead orthodoxy never crosses the street with the intention of pointing a sinner to the Savior. It is too respectable for that. It is too dignified. It is too cold.

HYPER-CALVINISM AND DEAD ORTHODOXY

It is humbling to think that God uses sin-prone vessels to convey the gospel to the lost. You could even describe it as strange or preposterous. Who are we to carry such a message? Our hands are tainted with sin. Our lips are unclean. Our minds are finite and warped with ungodly passions. But God did not determine to use angels as His conveyors of the gospel. He uses Christians, warts and all. This demonstrates God's wisdom, because if someone is converted, we know it was not us who did it. It also demonstrates God's power since we know we could never make a person into a new creation. The power is in the gospel, not the "gospelizer." When someone is converted, all glory belongs to God, not the one who shared it. Yet God does use people as means to save souls.

Dead orthodoxy believes all of this. After all, dead orthodoxy is orthodox. It believes God uses means to convert the lost. But the way dead orthodoxy operates reveals something different. Dead orthodoxy's heart shows otherwise. Dead orthodoxy does not evangelize. It does not share the gospel with lost people, and it frowns at those who do.

We can better understand such a frame of mind by exploring what is called *hyper-Calvinism*. Hyper-Calvinism as a community is relatively non-existent in our day. There are pockets of card-carrying hyper-Calvinists here and there, but with few exceptions, it is almost unheard of anymore. Even those who deny the free offer of the gospel would, if pressed, refuse to believe themselves to be hyper-Calvinists. They would agree that God uses the means of evangelism to save the elect, despite obvious inconsistencies in other areas.

The same is not true for every era of the church, however. As recently as the eighteenth century, hyper-Calvinism could be found in countries where the Reformation had seen significant success. England has the most famous example. In 1785, the Northamptonshire Baptist Association met to discuss Matthew 28:18-20: *And Jesus came and said to them, "All authority in heaven and on earth has been given to me. Go therefore and make disciples of all nations, baptizing them in the name of the Father and of the Son and of the Holy Spirit, teaching them to observe all that I have commanded you. And behold, I am with you always, to the end of the age.*"

The question was raised whether this passage of Scripture, now known as *the Great Commission*, meant that the gospel should be taken to the lost all over the world. For modern readers, this seems like a silly thing to ask. Of course it does, we would say. Even dead orthodoxy would agree. But it was not always as obvious. The future father of missions, William Carey, was at that meeting, and he proposed that the pastors discuss whether Matthew 28 gave a clear command to take the gospel to the nations. John Collett Ryland, pastor of a nearby church, rebuked Carey: "You are a miserable enthusiast for asking such a question. . . . What? Can you preach in Arabic, in Persian, in Hindustani, in Bengali, that you think it your duty to send the gospel to the heathens?" He then followed with perhaps the most regrettable rebuke in church history: "Young man, sit down. When God pleases to convert the heathen, He will do it without your aid or mine."[24]

That we do not have very many John Collett Rylands among us today is all very encouraging. It looks like we are in the clear. But are we? There are not many who would argue that the Great Commission passages are no longer in effect today, but does that mean such beliefs are not widespread among us? Ryland and others were *theoretical* hyper-Calvinists, meaning hyper-Calvinism was part of their doctrine. That is not our challenge. Our doctrine is sounder than Ryland's regarding evangelism and missions. We know the gospel should go to all the nations. We know it should go to the lost who are caught up in the LGBTQ cult or

---

24   Michael A. G. Haykin, "Hyper-Calvinism and the Theology of John Gill," *Credo Magazine*, September 2019, https://credomag.com/wp-content/uploads/2019/10/Hyper-Calvinism-and-the-theology-of-John-Gill.pdf.

the Roman Catholics who venerate Mary. The challenge for us is *functional* or practical hyper-Calvinism, which we can more simply describe as dead orthodoxy. In fact, for evangelism, dead orthodoxy's results are just as perilous as hyper-Calvinism's, if not more so, because they are more subtle and deceptive.

I am not suggesting that only Calvinists fall into the error of dead orthodoxy regarding evangelism. There are just as many non-Calvinistic Christians and churches who are apathetic about souls and evangelism as there are Calvinists. In all my years of public evangelism, I have received more complaints from nominal Christians than I have Calvinists, so the problem is more widespread than any one circle or denomination. That is because dead orthodoxy is more widespread than any one circle or denomination. But even though dead orthodoxy will affirm the importance of evangelism on paper, it often falls short when it comes to the challenging part of practicing it.

WHY EVANGELISM IS DIFFICULT

The reason Mr. Formalist does not evangelize is because evangelism requires more than a shell of religion. It requires affection and warmth for the lost and a love for God's glory. It is willing to risk losing respectability and reputation in the eyes of the lost. It is willing to crucify its desire to have worldly esteem. If I share the gospel with someone who is lost, the person might see me as backward, fundamentalist, radical, bigoted, or just plain weird. Perhaps worse, it can expose me to trouble at work, with the law, or with my family. In some countries, it could lead to imprisonment or death. Any Christian shrinks in the face of such possibilities, but a Christian is empowered by the Holy Spirit, so he has supernatural strength to overcome such challenges. Dead orthodoxy, though, has been calcified into silence. It is willing to go with Christ up to a certain point and no further.

Paul is one of the best examples we have of warm orthodoxy and evangelism. He gives us a taste of his urgency for souls in 1 Corinthians 9 with his use of the word *win*. The term *soul winning* might suggest people knocking on doors with their Bibles or handing out tracts on a street corner, practices very brackish to dead orthodoxy. But we need to unpack this phrase. First, soul winning is the opposite of passive. It is something active and vigorous. Winning is not for someone dead or frozen. Second, in some circles, the idea of winning souls can sound too man-centered, putting too much emphasis on Paul as the winner of souls when we know the Bible teaches that *salvation belongs to the* LORD (Jonah 2:9). But Paul knows what he is saying. Paul is the one who gave us the great predestinarian passages of Romans 9 and Ephesians 1. Dead orthodoxy tends to want to be more Calvinistic than the Bible. For Paul, without question, God elects and predestines to salvation. But Paul just as adamantly emphasized the role of Christians in the salvation of those same souls. We are instruments. We are means to that end. Thus, Paul said he aimed to *win* souls.

For example, consider Paul's emphasis, throughout his letters, on *hearing*. Writing to the Romans, Paul said, *So faith comes from hearing, and hearing through the word of Christ* (Romans 10:17). When writing to the Thessalonians he said, *We also thank God constantly for this, that when you received the word of God, which you heard from us, you accepted it not as the word of men but as what it really is, the word of God, which is at work in you believers* (1 Thessalonians 2:13). Again, when writing to the Galatians, Paul asked, *Did you receive the Spirit by the works of the law or by hearing with faith?* (Galatians 3:2). To the Ephesians he said, *In him you also, when you heard the word of truth, the gospel of your salvation* (Ephesians 1:13). Hearing requires a speaker. It presupposes that a human being will engage with another human being and share with them the message of salvation.

In fact, Paul went further. He did not merely emphasize the importance of speaking to the lost about Jesus, but he said it was his life's work. But notice he did not mean only speaking to people. That is difficult enough, as anyone who has ever evangelized knows. But Paul wanted more. His aim was to win them, to capture them to Christ. Paul knew God was sovereign in salvation, but he also saw himself having a part to play when it came to the saving of souls. What is more, he wanted to make sure nothing hindered him from achieving this. His orthodoxy was anything but dead. It was outward oriented. *I have made myself a servant to all, that I might win more* (1 Corinthians 9:19). He wanted to *win Jews*, those *under the law*. He also wanted to *win the weak*. He had *become all things to all people, that by all means I might save some* (1 Corinthians 9:19-22).

Paul was thoroughly convinced he was a conduit by which people were won to God. He even told us that he sought to win souls in any or every way, *by all means*. This is not to say Paul compromised the gospel or his moral conduct in order to save people. It means he was willing to go out of his way to sacrifice ordinary customs and comforts so that people would be saved. This is what he meant in his letter to Timothy: *I endure everything for the sake of the elect, that they also may obtain the salvation that is in Christ Jesus with eternal glory* (2 Timothy 2:10). The elect are out there. They are brought in by our efforts. Did Paul believe in God's sovereignty in the salvation of the elect? Of course he did. Paul would have signed off on Westminster's statement that "these angels and men, thus predestinated and fore-ordained, are particularly and unchangeably designed, and their number so certain and definite that it cannot be either increased or diminished." ("WCF" 3.4). But rather than stifling his zeal or making him *dead*, it enflamed him.

We can also see this warmth when Paul spoke about his fellow countrymen, the Jews. It is no accident that the following statement serves as the introduction to the great statements about election that follow: *I am speaking the truth in Christ – I am not lying; my conscience bears me witness in the Holy Spirit – that I have great sorrow and unceasing anguish in my heart. For I could wish that I myself were accursed and cut off from Christ for the sake of my brothers, my kinsmen according to the flesh* (Romans 9:1-3). Such great sorrow for the lost catapulted him into one of the greatest missionary endeavors the world has ever known. This is rightly ordered orthodoxy. It is a melding together of doctrinal truth and warm affection.

Granted, in one sense, we cannot compare ourselves to Paul. God had endued him with a special unction of the Holy Spirit. He had unmatched fortitude, power, insight, and personal experience of God's power. He received direct and infallible revelation from God. But how often do we use such comparisons as an excuse to not evangelize? How often do we justify our own dead orthodoxy by claiming Paul's letters and the Acts of the Apostles are descriptive, not prescriptive? We think we should not expect to have the zeal of the early church. We should not expect to see God move in the same way and give the same success. We should not be as enthusiastic or as absorbed in these things. But this is an excuse, a cop out.

For example, it is well documented that God has often poured out His Spirit in a way powerfully similar to what happened in the first century. Read the descriptions of any of the genuine revivals of the past to see the power and success of the gospel. See how entire communities are changed in character and conversation and how people are crushed beneath the presence of God.[25] There have been hundreds or even thousands of men

---

25   For example, see Jonathan Edward's "A Faithful Narrative," as well as his "Distinguishing Marks" and his "Some Thoughts on the Revival." Also see chapter 7 of Matthew Everhard's book, *A Theology of Joy: Jonathan Edwards and Eternal Happiness in the Holy Trinity.*

in church history used by God in a way remarkably similar to the apostle Paul. No one else was an apostle in the same sense that Paul was, but he was not the only one who has been used mightily by God. And even if we are not as successful as Paul, we are told to imitate him (1 Corinthians 11:1). We are not Paul, but we can pray, share the gospel, and do what we can to *win souls* in the same way as he did. The same Holy Spirit indwells us, and we have the same gospel. Perhaps our problem is that our orthodoxy is more "orthodox" than Paul's.

Soul winning is a term that makes us uncomfortable. It assumes that we must be active in the work. Soul winning itself is uncomfortable. Our flesh screams out anytime we approach a lost person with the gospel. This is normal. Paul felt it too. He experienced weakness, fear, and trembling. But an orthodoxy that is warm and alive will lean on Christ in times of intimidation and devote itself to the business of winning souls. This is not to say Christians will have the same zeal or success as Paul, but why shouldn't we expect to? Shouldn't we want to? Shouldn't we plead to God for more warmth and fruit in our evangelistic labors? Dead orthodoxy folds its arms and shakes its head, but that is because it is dead and stiff. It lacks affection for souls and the glory of God.

THE DUTY OF EVANGELISM

This is why it can be helpful to see evangelism as a duty, as opposed to something we really love to do. We should love evangelism, but the reality is that we usually do not. Even evangelists find evangelism difficult. So how do we evangelize even when we do not want to, when it means we may lose respectability or social credit?

The answer is to simply do it whether we feel like it or not. Dead orthodoxy can do this as well, but motive will be the difference. Our love for Christ and our love for our neighbor compels us to share the gospel with them. We seek to obey Christ because we love Christ, especially in light of the gospel. The flesh is weak, but with God's help, we learn to crucify the flesh. We learn to not heed the counsel of the flesh.

Duty as a motive for evangelism may sound coarse or even legalistic. Seeing people saved and growing our churches seem more noble and biblical motives. They are noble and biblical motives, but they are not the only ones, and there are times when those noble motives will not be enough. The very nature of evangelism requires such a word as duty. In several respects, evangelism is different than any other Christian practice. It entails intentionally speaking to a lost person about Jesus and sin, even though as far as we can tell at the present time, the person has no love for Christ or hatred for sin. And despite our modern assumptions about man, biblically speaking, unless God is drawing them, we are sharing Jesus with someone who does not want to hear about Him. Evangelism is sharing the good news of Christ with a lost person and then calling that person to repent and believe the message. This is not always pleasant. What other Christian duty is like this? Evangelism is confrontational, uncomfortable, and a catalyst for awkward tension, regardless of how respectfully and gently we do it. This is why dead orthodoxy loathes it.

We can see evangelism's uniqueness when we compare it to worship services, another Christian duty. If the government were to come tell us we can no longer worship the Lord, we have a duty to do so anyway. It is the same with evangelism. Even if it were illegal, we would be obligated to do it. In both scenarios, the way we worship or the way we evangelize may be different than how we would ordinarily do things, but we would still do it. Even when evangelism is seen as offensive, distasteful, politically incorrect, or illegal, we are still called to do it. This will expose us to harassment and danger, which is why the word *duty* is so essential. It implies doing something despite the difficulty that ensues. And isn't that what makes evangelism so difficult? It necessarily brings about conflict.

We should not be rude or obnoxious when evangelizing or intentionally seek conflict. On the contrary, we should be respectful and aware of the context in which we are evangelizing. But even if the person we evangelize gets saved on the spot, there will now be conflict between the new believer and his old way of life and his relationships. And if he is not converted, there will now be conflict between him and us, whether it is open hostility or something more subtle. There is no neutrality in the gospel. When we share the gospel, it will cause a response – either to salvation or to further condemnation – and all because we opened our mouths about Jesus.

Isn't this why we get nervous before we evangelize? Perhaps *nervous* is too soft of a word. This is why we get downright terrified. We all have difficulty evangelizing. Our flesh does not want the conflict. We recoil from pushback or looking foolish. We are afraid we will not have answers to their objections. But we must do it anyway because our Lord commands us to do so. It is His method for saving souls. *Faith comes by hearing.*

The duty to evangelize is not for ministers only. It is for all who name the name of Christ. Every Christian is important to the work of evangelism whether they are ordained ministers or not. God uses His people in every walk of life to add to His church. Backlash against such a message has always been the norm, but so are conversions. We must not be silent about our Lord. We may lose friends or look silly because of it, but we must not be ashamed of the gospel.

This is one way to understand Christ's promise that *"everyone who acknowledges me before men, I also will acknowledge before my Father who is in heaven, but whoever denies me before men, I also will deny before my Father who is in heaven*" (Matthew 10:32-33). Christ was speaking of people who deny their Lord as an attempt to protect themselves from harm. Even in a culture where we are not actively martyred for our faith, we are still persecuted through societal isolation, loss of job, friends, or even family whenever we take seriously the command to evangelize the lost. In the following verse, Jesus promised that He did not come to bring peace to the earth but a sword (Matthew 10:34).

Dead orthodoxy considered George Whitefield, John Wesley, David Brainerd, Jonathan Edwards, and even William Carey to be embarrassments.[26] They were viewed as zealots and radicals. But these men were willing to be fools for Christ's sake, even when they scandalized the church. Consider John Ryland's response to the criticism of William Carey by other clergymen in their day: "I am almost worn out with grief at these foolish cavils against some of the best of my brethren, men of God, who are only hated because of their zeal."[27] Michael A. G. Haykin notes that one of the hurdles William Carey had to overcome was "the lack of support by fellow Christians in England."[28]

The expected responses to biblical evangelism should be reproach and scoffing. In some contexts, so are arrests, confiscation of property, or loss of life. In fact, why would we assume any other response? The world's eyes are veiled to the gospel (2 Corinthians 4:3). There are none who seek God (Romans 3:11). But these responses are exactly why a church culture permeated with dead orthodoxy will shirk this duty to evangelize.

The world will hate Christians, especially if they boldly evangelize. Christ Himself told us to expect it. But why do

---

26   Edwards especially points this out in *Religious Affections*. Also see Matthew Everhard's, *Holy Living: Jonathan Edwards's Seventy Resolutions for Living the Christian Life*.

27   Cited in A. de M. Chesterman, "The Journals of Daniel Brainerd and of William Carey," *The Baptist Quarterly* 19 (1961–62): 151–52.

28   Michael A. G. Haykin, *The Missionary Fellowship of William Carey* (Sanford, FL: Reformation Trust Publishing, 2018), 5.

Christians shy away from confrontation? The answer is easy. Dead orthodoxy. We want to protect ourselves from being looked down on or losing friends, even if this means not evangelizing. The flesh is enormously powerful.

R. C. Sproul noted that "Jesus's life was a storm of controversy. The apostles, like the prophets before them, could hardly go a day without controversy. Paul said that he debated daily in the marketplace. To avoid controversy is to avoid Christ."[29] Do we think that Paul, the prophets, or even Christ delighted to be harassed, maligned, and eventually killed for what they believed? Certainly, those were not enjoyable situations. So, what drove them to keep pressing on, regardless of ill health, prison, or loss of life? What must drive us on to evangelize, even when we do not feel like it, even when it might cause outrage or social inconvenience? The answer is a warm, living, and real orthodoxy.

The power of Christianity has always been its bold, uncompromising gospel proclamation. It has proclaimed the gospel directly into the teeth of the fiercest, most ruthless societies ever known to man. Despite the persecution this has brought on the church, Christians have always dug in and preached even harder. The surrounding culture considered early Christians aggressive and imprudent, even while other religions were taking steps to avoid persecution. There has always been a relentless zeal for gospel proclamation among God's people, demonstrated more brightly in some periods of church history than others; but it has been there, somewhere, even in the darkest ages. But it was not boldness for the sake of being bold that drove them on. It was not recklessness for the sake of recklessness. No matter how they felt or what the outcome would be, they carried on because the Master had told them to. Do we have

---

29   R. C. Sproul, *Essential Truths of the Christian Faith* (Carol Stream, IL: Tyndale House Publishers, 1992), xv.

this same mindset? Do we follow through with evangelism no matter how we feel about it?

IS WARM ORTHODOXY ENOUGH?

The practical outworking of dead orthodoxy is devastating. This is seen most clearly in evangelism. The stakes are nothing less than eternal souls. Those with a dead orthodoxy want to leave it to someone else to share the gospel with the people in their lives. They believe it is not their job, but rather the pastor, the evangelist, or outgoing individuals who are supposed to share the gospel. Dead orthodoxy closes the door on any environment or situation that might bring reproach, disrepute, shame, or embarrassment from the world, which is what usually happens when one actively shares the gospel.

Have you ever known this hesitancy? Have you blinked when faced with the opportunity to share the gospel? I imagine every Christian has, which is why we cannot say Christians who have not been faithful in evangelism are necessarily lost or have a dead orthodoxy. But we need to seek God's help, because to balk at or fail to share the gospel is an element of dead orthodoxy. People are disseminating false gospels around the world today, even to the people who are in our own lives. Who is going to bring the true gospel to them? We have orthodoxy, but if it is not living, it does not spread. Dead orthodoxy grows inward, festers, and begets more death. So where have we made excuses for our lack of evangelism? When have we delegated to others the task of evangelism? When has our fear of man kept us from evangelizing? Living things beget life, not death.

Luke gave us a good example of true orthodoxy in the story of the tombstone demoniac. After Christ healed him and put him *in his right mind* (Luke 8:35), the man wanted to go with Christ across the sea. He now loved Christ and wanted to be

with Him; he had the attitude of a believer. But Jesus told him
no. He could not go with Him yet. It is the same for us. It is not
yet time to behold Christ face to face. Neither is it time to rest
in the ivory tower of orthodoxy. Christ told the newly healed
man to *"return to your home, and declare how much God has
done for you"* (Luke 8:39). That is our call as Christians. Like
the demoniac, many of us do not have Bible degrees. We have
not been to evangelism conferences. We do not know much
theology or church history; but we know Christ, and we know
what Christ has done for our souls. We can certainly share that,
and an orthodoxy that is not dead will share it.

Christ was the only person who has ever had perfect theology, and His theology did not stifle His zeal. He was the greatest evangelist the world has ever known. After Adam sinned, it
was Christ who sought him out in the garden and uttered the
protoevangelium, or the first gospel (Genesis 3:15). God sought
out Abram while he was still a pagan. And most dramatically
of all, when the world was lying under a curse, Christ took on
flesh to save dead, grimy, malicious, and perverted souls. Having
been saved, we are now commanded to go to other souls with
the gospel. Christ continues to be the preeminent soul winner,
but in God's marvelous wisdom, He has determined to do this
through His church.

After Peter and John were arrested and ordered not to speak
of Jesus, they insisted: *"We cannot but speak of what we have
seen and heard"* (Acts 4:20). If our orthodoxy is alive, we will
insist on the same thing, even if the one complaining is our
own flesh. With God's grace we will tell our flesh, "Hush. Be
quiet. We are going to speak of what we have seen and heard.
We must go speak of the marvelous gospel of Jesus Christ." For
most churches plagued by dead orthodoxy, evangelism means
putting out a stack of confessions and creeds and some books
by Calvin and John Owen and then waiting for the lost to come

stampeding in. But it does not work like that. We must go to them. *How are they to hear without someone preaching? And how will they preach unless they are sent?* (Romans 10:14-15).

STUDY QUESTIONS

1. Do you agree with the above assessment that evangelism is a duty?

2. Are there times when your evangelism has been lacking? In what areas has it been strong?

3. Recount an experience you had in which you overcame fear in order to share the gospel with someone. What was a time when you succumbed to fear and did not share the gospel?

4. Has hyper-Calvinism persisted in your circles? How can we make sure it does not gain prominence?

CHAPTER 6

WHEN CHRISTIANS BECOME DEISTS

Dead orthodoxy has a sister. She is just as ugly as Mr. Formalist and Respectable Christianity, but unfortunately, may be even more popular. Her name is *Deism*. She also goes by the name *Rationalism*. More recently, she has even gone around under the guise of *Hyper-Cessationism*.

Deism is the belief that God created the world but has chosen to have limited or no involvement in it. Rationalism, for our purposes, is similar; everything can be explained or *rationalized* without any reference to the supernatural. It is the idea that the supernatural is superfluous. It is unnecessary. It posits that human reason is sufficient to obtain eternal truths. Similarly, truths that are not eternal can be obtained through experience of the physical world, which is further refined and articulated by the scientific method. Hence, there is no need for God or the supernatural. We can trust only what the mind can observe or rationalize. The world is a closed system, and not even God can violate its laws.

This is where dead orthodoxy rears its head. It would never

agree with such sentiments on paper. It is orthodox, after all. It believes in God. It believes in the supernatural. It believes that God has a unique place when it comes to His relationship with the natural world. Most of the time it would believe in miracles and the healing of people through prayer. It may even believe in certain types of revival, such as occurred in the First Great Awakening. But its beliefs are merely theoretical. Practically, dead orthodoxy operates as though there is no God, or at the very best, that God's operations are limited and never unusual.

HOW TO SPOT A DEIST

How do we identify deism or rationalism in ourselves or in others? We can ask ourselves some questions. Do we doubt God can heal or do miracles? Do we expect God to answer our prayers? Is God just as real to us as the things we perceive with our senses? Do we doubt the accounts of Muslims having visions which then lead them to the Lord? Do we doubt the veracity of revivals under Edwards, Whitefield, Wesley, Gilbert Tennent, Asahel Nettleton, or more recently those in Civil War camps or at the Wall Street prayer meeting in 1857? Do we doubt the prophetic nature of dreams of such men as John Flavel, a prominent seventeenth-century Puritan minister? Flavel himself was a believer in such dreams: "Mr. Flavel replied that he expected much trouble because of his dream the night before, adding, that when he had such representations made to him in his sleep, they seldom or never failed. Accordingly, they were overtaken by a dreadful tempest."[30] Do we roll our eyes when we hear of the prophetic insight of men like John Knox and Jan Huss, the latter apparently predicting both the rise of Luther and the timing of his appearance?[31]

---

30   "The Life of John Flavel," *The Works of John Flavel*, vol.1, (republished Carlisle, PA: Banner of Truth, 1968), 124–25.
31   See *The Life of John Knox* by Thomas M'Crie and *The Scots Worthies* by John Howie.

Scottish Covenanter Samuel Rutherford wrote about such men. Considering Rutherford's substantial role in the Westminster Assembly, out of which came one of Protestantism's most influential confessions,[32] his words are worth giving in full:

There is a third revelation of some particular men who have foretold things to come, even since the ceasing of the Canon, as John Huss, Wycliffe, Luther have foretold things to come and they certainly fell out, and in our nation of Scotland, M. George Wishart foretold that Cardinal Beaton should not come out alive at the gates of the Castle of St. Andrews but that he should die a shameful death; and he was hanged over the window that he did look out when he saw the man of God burnt. Mr. Knox prophesied of the hanging of the Lord of Grange. Mr. John Davidson uttered prophecies, known to many of the kingdom, and diverse preachers in England have done the like.[33]

We see here that Rutherford clearly considered Knox and others to be prophets. This will be surprising to some because Rutherford was a prominent Presbyterian and a contributor to the "Westminster Confession of Faith," which is where the term *cessationism* comes from.

Perhaps the most startling example of the strange and unusual in the seventeenth-century Reformed world came at the hands of John Welch, son-in-law of John Knox and another notable Presbyterian minister. After a young nobleman died, he was raised to life two days later through the prayers of John Welch. This is recorded in *The Scots Worthies*, published by

32   The Westminster Standards (including the Westminster Confession of Faith, Larger and Shorter Catechism, and the Directory for Public Worship).
33   Samuel Rutherford, *A Survey of the Spiritual Antichrist* (London:1648), 42.

Banner of Truth. Because of the oddity of such an account, it is also worth giving in full:

So the physicians are let to work, who pinched him with pincers in the fleshy parts of his body, and twisted a bowstring about his head with great force, but no sign of life appearing in him, the physicians pronounced him stark dead, and then there was no more delay to be made; yet Mr. Welch begged of them once more that they would but step into the next room for an hour or two and leave him with the dead youth; and this they granted. Then Mr. Welch fell down before the pallet and cried to the Lord with all his might, and sometimes looked upon the dead body, continuing in wrestling with the Lord, till at length the dead youth opened his eyes and cried out to Mr. Welch, whom he distinctly knew, "O Sir, I am all whole, but my head and legs"; and these were the places they had sore hurt with their pinching.

When Mr. Welch perceived this, he called upon his friends and showed them the dead young man restored to life again, to their great astonishment. . . . This story the nobleman himself communicated to his friends in Ireland.[34]

How does what we read here compare with our view of reality? We see such things in the Scriptures, but do they really take place in the same way today? Do we believe the Lord caused an iron ax-head to float? Did He part the Red Sea in two? Did Jonah live

---

34 John Howie, *The Scots Worthies* (1870; republished Carlisle, PA: Banner of Truth, 1995), 45. There are also reports in other places of Ebenezer Erskine's mother being raised from the dead after being buried in the ground.

in the belly of a fish, and was Lazarus raised from the dead? To assume such things are too extraordinary in our day would seem to go beyond what people such as Flavel and Rutherford believed. It would go beyond what John Welch saw. So, the question is why have today's Christians come to such deistic conclusions? Why has modern Christianity, especially in the conservative and confessional world, swung to such a radical position as it pertains to how God moves and operates in our world today?

This is not an argument for continuationism as opposed to cessationism or the other way around. This is more fundamental than that. Christians in the West are in constant danger of being overly rationalistic because of the prevalence of rationalism, materialism, and scientism in our culture today. We are in danger of being deists without knowing it. We do not typically deal with the problems of animism and voodoo in the West. We face the problems of atheism, Darwinian evolution, and secular humanism. We deal with materialism and the ramifications of Enlightenment thought. Because these views are so dominant in the culture around us, whether we admit it or not, deism inevitably finds a home in our hearts and in our churches. Our extremes tend toward the denial of the supernatural, miracles, the devil, and the unusual outpourings of God's Spirit that we see throughout church history.

Syncretism is not only a blending of animistic and pagan religions with Christianity. Syncretism also occurs when we blend our western religions of evolution, humanism, and scientism with the Christian faith. We will not tackle here such doctrinal syncretism as theistic evolution, liberation theology, or woke theology, but rather the practical – or orthopraxy – side of things. After all, orthodoxy is not the problem. Dead orthodoxy is. Our doctrines are fine, but our practice is where the problem lies. So where do we find practical syncretism in churches and individuals whose Christianity is otherwise orthodox?

HYPER-CESSATIONISM AND REVIVAL[35]

Cessationism proper is the belief that God revealed His will in the Old Testament and in the days of the apostles in a way that *ceased* with the completion of the canon. In its most basic form, cessationism says that God has stopped giving any new doctrine and/or new ethics. It is the belief that there is no more canon to be given, and God will not give any more *infallible* revelation that is on the same level as Scripture itself.

I do not intend to contribute extensively to the debate over cessationism and continuationism here. Much has already been written. However, I am purporting here that popular treatments of cessationism often swing to an extreme that the writers of the "Westminster Confession," as one example of cessationists, never intended. I am deeply troubled by some of the assumptions that the term *cessationist* now seems to carry. Cessationism has morphed into something dark and suffocating. It has become a thick, wet blanket used to smother anything that hints of the supernatural. Contemporary proponents of this type of cessationism seem to think and teach that the term means God has no interaction with us apart from His Word and that all miracles except for conversion have ceased. At the very least, claims of the miraculous are to be looked at with disdain and doubt. They teach that most spiritual gifts have ceased. There are no more *signs and wonders* (Acts 5:12). But such a view is not consistent with historical cessationism. It is a type of contemporary distortion that can only be described as *hyper-cessationism*, and its consequences are dire. J. I. Packer would seem to agree with my assessment, writing to Wayne Grudem that the idea of "personal informative revelation . . . was the standard Puritan view, as I have observed it – they weren't cessationists in the Richard Gaffin sense."[36]

---

35   Much of this section can be found in my articles at Reformation21.org
36   See Wayne Grudem's *The Gift of Prophecy in the New Testament and Today*, rev. ed. (Wheaton, IL: Crossway, 2000), 356.

We could define a hyper-cessationist, then, as a person who is not just a cessationist but who also aggressively tries to disprove or undermine reports of the contemporary moving of the Spirit; who is automatically skeptical of the miraculous, including but not limited to revival, healing, dreams, and visions; and whose worldview is closer to functional deism or rationalism despite theoretically denying such. Generally, it means a person who has gone beyond what the divines intended in the cessationist clause of the "Westminster Confession of Faith," which as we will see, was meant to protect against claims of new doctrine and ethics, not signs, wonders, impressions, and gifts (including prophecy), assuming they are consistent with and ordinarily mediated through the Holy Scriptures.

Popular treatments of cessationism rarely if ever nuance this, so most people in the cessationist camp are left thinking that God simply never makes use of dreams, angelic visits, or prophetic motions. Some even believe God no longer works miracles other than conversion. This hard or hyper-cessationism ultimately boxes God off from intervention in His world. The implications of this are drastic. Without realizing it, we have become more deistic than Christian. We have become materialists, intellectualists, and rationalists. Not only can everything be explained in terms of the natural, but we also do not expect or even desire to see anything unusual or supernatural. This is why people in these circles often reject revival and healing or are, at the very least, very suspicious about it.

SCIENTISM AND CHRISTIANITY

Dead orthodoxy is also an explanation for why theological novelties such as theistic evolution are able to take root even in otherwise conservative churches. For example, when the scientific community comes out with some theory that would seem to discredit the

Scriptures, our first instinct is to tinker with our interpretations of the Bible rather than to question the scientists. I am not saying that the scientific community has some underlying agenda to discredit the Scriptures, nor am I suggesting that science has no value when it comes to understanding the natural world. But *science* is a nebulous term, and the theories of science change as often as the weather. The working hypotheses of today's scientific community will look radically different than those of tomorrow's community. Science is helpful, but the experiments conducted are reliant on the presuppositions of those conducting them. Unbelieving scientists will interpret their findings and even base their experiments on the idea that there is no supernatural explanation for things. This presupposition automatically disqualifies any possibility of a young earth, as one example, or a universal flood, as another. Thus, the only explanation for what we see in the natural world today becomes that of Darwinian evolution: species randomly evolving into higher, more complex forms over a long period of time. This theory necessitates millions of years, and thus calculations of the natural realm are conducted with that in mind.

What does this have to do with our topic? This mentality automatically rejects anything abnormal, unusual, or miraculous as an explanation for what happens in the material realm. It sees explanations that depend upon the supernatural as sophomoric. We begin to see it as an excuse or even cheating to believe that we must leave room for the supernatural or explain things through the lens of God's intervention whenever we interpret things in the natural world. But why do we assume that is cheating? Why do we feel those explanations are inferior to the type that seeks to explain phenomena without God? Because the Enlightenment has told us so. The scientists have told us so. Our secular humanist worldview and education have told us so.

Thus, rationalism has come to dictate how we think about

things, and even Christians are prone to go along with it. Christians will begin to doubt the Scriptures when it comes to the age of the earth, whether the flood was universal, or whether all the miracles we read about could have happened as presented. If revival, miracles, and the supernatural cannot be accounted for by the scientific community, they are quickly dismissed as foolish, excessive, and anti-scientific, even by Christians. This applies not only to how we interpret the Bible but also to how we view such things today. Any talk of miracles, revival, or unusual demonstrations of the Holy Spirit are immediately jettisoned because they cannot be explained by our neat and tidy theology or by our materialistic worldview.

REVIVAL AND RATIONALISM

Jonathan Edwards was someone who suffered the wrath of dead orthodoxy. When a powerful work of God appeared among his congregation, the Christian community was divided. Was this really of God, or was it mere enthusiasm?

Edwards was balanced enough to recognize the dangers of emotionalism and fanaticism, which are different than emotion and fervency.[37] But he also recognized that right theology does produce emotions such as joy, love, warmth, and supernatural power. Sometimes, when such emotions are evidenced in an unusual way, there will be excesses that should be curbed and confronted. For example, Paul does this with the church in Corinth. Their problem was not deadness. It was excessive exuberance and disorder caused by emotionalism. Genuine revivals often have a counterfeit component, such as fanaticism, but it does not mean that the revival itself is not of God.

---

37   For example, Edwards has a wonderful concept of the affections in his *Religious Affections*. They are not *emotions* but rather the soul's disposition toward or away from the things of the Lord, or inclinations. The change of one's affections is part of conversion. Thanks to Matthew Everhard for pointing this out to me.

Edwards understood this and tried to articulate it to the staid and respectable congregations who were mortified by what was going on. Edwards reasoned that even Christians in the grip of genuine revival will wrestle with sin and limitations in their wisdom. These Christians, in the grip of something fervent and joyful, are bound to express such joy in odd and even sinful ways. There are sinful extremes in anything, even revival. There can be excesses of emotion, enthusiasm, and even belief, and because Christians are not made of spirit only, but body and spirit, it is natural that people swoon or cry when God's Spirit falls on them, however odd this will appear to us in the moment.

But the other side of the coin also has a sinful extreme. The problem of dead orthodoxy is that there is an excess of skepticism and caution regarding any kind of spiritual activity. Because of certain excesses that have cropped up in times of revival, there is a reluctance and even a disdain for anything out of the ordinary. Dead orthodoxy walks around in perpetual doubt regarding any claim to the supernatural. Speaking of such a state, Martyn Lloyd-Jones asked, "Is there not this appalling danger that we are just content because we have correct beliefs? And we have lost the life, the vital thing, the power, the thing that really makes worship worship, which is in Spirit and truth?"[38] Lloyd-Jones went on to say that "dislike of enthusiasm is to quench the Spirit" and that "this charge of enthusiasm is the one that has always been brought against people who have been most active in a period of revival."[39] In another place he said, "There are churches that are orthodox but absolutely dead because they are so afraid of false excitement and the excesses of certain spiritual movements that they quench and hinder the Spirit and deny the true."[40] That is the dead orthodoxy we are describing here.

Is this true of us? Where have we dampened the fire of God's

---

38   Martyn Lloyd-Jones, *Revival* (Wheaton, IL: Crossway, 1987), 72.
39   Ibid., 72–73.
40   Lloyd-Jones, *Revival*, 78.

Spirit because it did not quite fit the mold we are comfortable with? Excesses and unhealthy exuberances should be curbed and even dismissed, but the danger for doctrinally sound churches is not excessive enthusiasm – it is no enthusiasm whatsoever. We think we are above emotions because we are intellectual. We are sophisticated. We have right doctrine. We have read all the big theological books. We have long ago shed the uncouth shouts of "Amen!" in the church service. We have been liberated from any fanaticism. This is the same as admitting we are orthodox but frozen. We are orthodox, but we lack warmth. We have light but no heat.

Many orthodox churches illustrate this by their approach to ordination for prospective ministers. There is a remarkably high bar when it comes to academic and theological training, but the bar is comparatively nonexistent when it comes to the spiritual life of the prospective minister. He is ruthlessly examined on his knowledge of theology, church history, Greek and Hebrew, the English Bible, sacraments, and church polity. He is expected to have at least two degrees, one of them a postgraduate degree in theology. There is nothing wrong with this, but yet, there could be. How often does a minister's prayer life collapse beneath the demands of academic rigor? How often does excessive time in academia's ivory tower quench the warmth of the Holy Spirit?

Ideally, extensive study of theology leads to more and more worship. This sometimes happens, but often, there is a drying out of the soul. Our spirit languishes and grows arid. Just as problematic, the minister grows too accustomed to his study. He loses touch with the life of the spirit, prayer, evangelism, and the miraculous. Those things are not found in books. How often are prospective ministers questioned about this by their credential committees, presbyteries, or board of elders? Does the church ever address the prospective minister's prayer life, his growth or lack of growth in holiness, his experiences of seeing prayers answered? Do they ask for evidence that his Christianity is not just academic? I am not saying this is always the case, but I think any honest reader in such circles will admit that there is a heavy imbalance toward knowledge and very little demand of the experiential.

WESTMINSTER DIVINES AND CESSATIONISM

As we saw with John Flavel, even those who are considered cessationists would object to the contemporary extremes of dead orthodoxy as it pertains to the work of the Holy Spirit. For example, it has been well documented that many of the Westminster divines believed that dreams, angelic visitations, and prophetic impulses and motions could all still have a role in the ordinary lives of Christians.[41] For example, John Owen was representative when he stated, "To say God does not or may not send his angels to any of his saints, to communicate his mind to them as to some particulars of their duty according to his word or to foreshadow to them his own approaching work, seems to unwarrantably limit the Holy One of Israel."[42] William Bridge, a Westminster divine, wrote: "But, you will say, may not God speak by extraordinary visions and revelations in these days of ours? Yes, without all doubt he may: God is not to be limited; he may speak in what way he pleases."[43] Richard Baxter agreed with both Owen and Bridge, but he expressed his views more candidly than either: "It is possible that God may make new revelations to particular persons about their duties, events, or matters of fact, in subordination to the Scripture, either by inspiration, vision, apparition, or voice."[44]

---

41 For example, see Poythress's article at https://frame-poythress.org/modern-spiritual-gifts-as-analogous-to-apostolic-gifts-affirming-extraordinary-works-of-the-spirit-within-cessationist-theology/, Milne's book, *The Westminster Confession of Faith and the Cessation of Special Revelation*, and De Young's post at https://www.thegospelcoalition.org/blogs/kevin-deyoung/the-puritans-strange-fire-cessationism-and-the-westminster-confession/.

42 John Owen, *Exposition on the Book of Hebrews*, vol. 3 (Edinburgh: Banner of Truth, 1991), 250.

43 William Bridge, *The Works of the Rev. Bridge*, vol. 1, (London: Thomas Tegg, 1845), 401–402.

44 Richard Baxter, *A Christian Directory* (London: 1673), 909.

Closer to Jonathan Edwards, both geographically and chrono-logically, was Cotton Mather who said about his grandfather: "Increase Mather did no less than three Times as the Year, 1678, was coming on, very Publicly Declare, That he was verily Persuaded, a very Mortal Disease would shortly break in, and the Slain of the Lord would be many. Some of his Friends were troubled at him for it. But when the Year 1678 was come on, we saw the Mortal Disease. The Small-Pox broke in."[45] George Gillespie said that John Knox, John Welsh, Robert Bruce, and others were "more than ordinary pastors and teachers, even holy prophets receiving extraordinary revelations from God, and foretelling strange and remarkable things, which did accordingly come to pass punctually to the great admiration of all who knew the particulars."[46]

Quotes such as these have led Kevin DeYoung to conclude that "without a doubt, the "Westminster Confession of Faith" teaches cessationism, but it is a cessationism which requires considerable nuance and allows for supernatural surprises so long as they are working with and through the Word of God."[47] In what may be the most scholarly treatment of cessationism in the Reformed tradition, Garnet Howard Milne concludes, "Many of the authors of the 'WCF' accepted that 'prophecy' continued in their time, and a number of them apparently believed that disclosure of God's will through dreams, visions, and angelic communication remained possible."[48] This is why the Westminster divines, who gave us the section on the ces-sation of certain types of revelation, also wrote "WCF" 5.3:

---

45   Cotton Mather, *Parentator: Memoirs of Remarkables in the Life and the Death of the Ever-Memorable Dr. Increase Mather* (Boston: B. Green, 1724), 189–91.

46   George Gillespie, *The Works of George Gillespie*, vol. 2, ed. David Meek (Edmonton: SWRB, 1991), 30.

47   Kevin DeYoung, "The Puritans, Strange Fire, Cessationism, and the Westminster Confession," *The Gospel Coalition Blogs, The Gospel Coalition*, October 18, 2013, https://www.thegospelcoalition.org/blogs/kevin-deyoung/the-puritans-strange-fire-cessationism-and-the-westminster-confession.

48   Garnet Howard Milne, *The Westminster Confession of Faith and the Cessation of Special Revelation* (Eugene, OR: Paternoster, 2007), xv.

"God, in his ordinary providence, maketh use of means, yet is free to work without, above, and against them, at his pleasure."

So, what about the Puritans' and Scottish Covenanters' practice of prophesying? In general, the Puritans and Covenanters seemed to see prophecy as God's Spirit impressing intuitions on them as it pertained to specific tasks, duties, insights, or even upcoming circumstances. These were unusual but regular enough to find a place in many of their writings. It is also well documented that Spurgeon seemed to have exercised this "gift" on several occasions.

Importantly, again, they did not believe these prophecies conveyed new doctrine, new ethics, or infallible revelation on the same level as Scripture. They were cessationists in that regard. But they did recognize the existence of God-given "revelation" as it pertained to specific situations. This is what J. I. Packer meant when he said: "Personal informative revelation was the standard Puritan view as I have observed it."

But such a view begs the question: how can one receive prophetic revelation from God that is not infallible and does not compete with the sufficiency of Scripture? Vern Poythress gives the best answer I have come across: "I explain how partly by distinguishing teaching content from circumstantial content. Teaching content must not add to Scripture but can only rephrase what is already there in Scripture. Circumstantial content has the same status as information received through a long-distance telephone call – that is, it has no special claim to authority. It is therefore obvious that neither type of content threatens the sufficiency of Scripture."[49]

We could quibble over whether this is the gift of prophecy or not, but it seems clear that the *circumstantial* usage was a recognized fact in the seventeenth-century Reformed world, and

---

49 Vern Poythress, "Modern Spiritual Gifts as Analogous to Apostolic Gifts: Affirming Extraordinary Works of the Spirit within Cessationist Theology," *The Works of John Frame & Vern Poythress* (blog), June 6, 2012, https://frame-poythress.org/modern-spiritual-gifts-as-analogous-to-apostolic-gifts-affirming-extraordinary-works-of-the-spirit-within-cessationist-theology/.

they did use the word prophecy to describe it. This is interesting because, as mentioned, out of this environment came the "Westminster Confession of Faith" and the "Second London Baptist Confession of Faith" of 1689.

Such views of the miraculous and supernatural were not only common in the Reformed and Protestant world, but they were also especially abundant in the first centuries of the New Testament church. For instance, the aged Augustine reported a litany of miracles and extraordinary events that took place either in his city or near to it:

> A miracle that happened at Milan while I was there, when a blind man had his sight restored. . . . I have been concerned that such accounts should be published because I saw that signs of divine power like those of the older days were frequently occurring in modern times too. . . . Many miracles have occurred there [at Hippo] and to my certain knowledge, many miracles have occurred there which are not recorded in the published documents and nearly seventy of these documents have been produced at the time of writing.[50]

Irenaeus tells us in his *Against Heresies* that a man was brought back to life after having been dead.[51] Justin Martyr, Jerome, Basil the Great, and other church fathers spoke of exorcisms and strange prophecies coming to pass. Again, this is not an argument for continuationism in contrast to cessationism. That would require a different kind of book. This is a general examination pertaining to the world of the supernatural. If certain cultures and churches err on the side of enthusiasm,

---

50 Augustine, *City of God*, 22.8
51 Irenaeus, *Against Heresies*, 2.31.2

fanaticism, and hyper-gullibility, others fall into the ditch of materialism and hyper-skepticism. Many churches in the West find themselves in this situation.

As we consider what we have just read, and there is much more written on this subject, what is our understanding of revival, angelic communication, dreams, and visions? How do we feel about the above phenomena? Do they make us squeamish? Do we consider them dubious? Should we reject them mostly or completely out of hand? If we say yes without reservation, it could be a sign of dead orthodoxy.

To what extent such things happen today, or even whether they happen at all, is a reasonable enough discussion. But what are we saying about God when we flatly deny or scoff at the idea of God intervening in ways mentioned above? What are we saying about ourselves to assume we can do without such powerful workings of God? What are we saying when we assume that our proper and philosophical Christianity is the right expression of the faith, in contrast to most of church history, the Scriptures, and even most churches and Christians in the world today?

It is necessary to test the spirits, especially in times of perceived revival or supernatural movements, but it is improper to presume that God is unlikely to do these things based merely on our experience living in a Western world, heavily permeated with rationalistic and evolutionary patterns of thought. We are saturated in Enlightenment and anti-supernatural paradigms, even from the womb. Is it possible that Western Christians are the ones who have it wrong? Is it not odd that except for the West, the rest of the Christian world is "charismatic" in their expressions of faith? Other places in the world need caution when it comes to excesses in their emotion and exuberance, but for us in the West, we need to exercise caution when it comes to our rationalism.

LOUD AND RITZY IS NOT THE WAY

This is not to say we should have loud, ecstatic, and disorderly expressions of Christian living or worship. This is a call to balance. If we have gravitated toward a non-experiential view of the Christian life, we need to come back to the center. If we have gravitated to a disorderly and erratic view of the Christian life, we also need to return to the center. But in the West, especially in churches that are orthodox, our imbalance tends to be toward the dry, stale, and even dead expression of faith. Orthodoxy tends to lean more toward hard-cessationism, not charismania. Even becoming aware of this will help to stabilize our Christian life and worship.

Christians are not called to be deists. We are not called to be rationalists in the scientific sense of the word. We believe in a God who is intimately involved in His creation, including in the ways He communicates and deals with His people and as well as in the extraordinary, incalculable way He created all things from nothing in the space of six ordinary, twenty-four-hour days. This may militate against current scientific theories, but such theories are governed by presuppositions that conflict with the Scripture's own presuppositions.

Each Christian must decide which account of reality he will follow. We know scientific theories are fickle. Unlike the Word of God, they change with every generation: *The grass withers, the flower fades, but the word of our God will stand forever* (Isaiah 40:8). Have we quenched the Spirit by our disbelief in revival, the miraculous, or powerful workings of the supernatural? Have we become imbalanced in our view of the wonderful works of God and lived as functional deists?

In these days, when evil seems to be increasing on every side, we need more of God's unction, power, and Spirit, not less. We need to hold to the historical and more moderate understanding of cessationism, not its ugly stepsister that has been dragging her stale, dry, cumbersome broom across Reformed and conservative churches everywhere, sweeping away anything that suggests too much life and vigor. Hamlet could have been speaking to hyper-cessationists when he said: "There are more things in heaven and earth than are dreamt of in your philosophy." In the words of the "Westminster Confession": "God, in his ordinary providence, maketh use of means, yet is free to work without, above, and against them, at his pleasure" (5.3).

STUDY QUESTIONS

1. When has the supernatural made you uncomfortable? When has a sham or counterfeit presentation of the supernatural made you uncomfortable?

2. What are your thoughts about Muslims having dreams that lead to their apparent conversion?

3. In what areas have naturalistic or materialistic presuppositions influenced you?

4. How do you explain to an unbeliever the miraculous passages in the Bible, such as the floating iron ax-head or a fish swallowing Jonah?

CHAPTER 7

PRAYERLESSNESS

The best way to gauge our dependency on God is to examine our prayer life. Similarly, the way to gauge if our orthodoxy is dead is by the same route – our prayer life. A dead faith is not a praying faith. This is why Calvin called prayer "the chief exercise of faith."[52] Dead orthodoxy may utter a few phrases in a mechanical or rote fashion, but it knows nothing of genuine communion with God.

The same is true of churches. A spirit of prayer will mark a church whose orthodoxy is alive. Does the church have healthy, vibrant prayer meetings? Does the church have sincere, heartfelt expressions of prayer both in public worship and in private meetings? Does the church in general seem to understand its desperate dependency on God? When she faces financial trials, division, or a loss of people, does she resort to more prayer and fasting or to the latest gimmicks in the business world?

Prayer at its basic level is the acknowledgement that we need God. It is a thirsting for God. This is why Jesus condemned rote

---

52   See Calvin's title of Book III of the *Institutes*, chapter 20.

or formulaic praying. Such prayer contradicts the very purpose of prayer, which is to draw near to God and for God to draw near to the believer. Rote prayer is repetition without feeling. There is no wonder or awe. There is no expectation. There is no desperation. Dead orthodoxy can go through the motion of praying, but it does not know what the heart of prayer is after. Jesus said as much in the Sermon on the Mount: *"And when you pray, you must not be like the hypocrites. For they love to stand and pray in the synagogues and at the street corners, that they may be seen by others. Truly, I say to you, they have received their reward"* (Matthew 6:5).

Jesus was not condemning the public nature of prayer since He Himself prayed publicly on several occasions (Matthew 14:19; 15:36). He was condemning their motive for praying; they cared more about being seen by man than by God. This is why He said in the same sermon to *shut the door* when you pray (Matthew 6:6). As far as possible, close yourself off to distractions, applause, or any affection that takes away from the reality that you are in God's presence, speaking with Him. This is why people close their eyes when praying. Scripture does not mandate that we close our eyes to pray, but closing our eyes allows us to shut out external distractions. It is an attempt to focus more exclusively on God. Prayer is about shutting the door to everything except communing with God and bringing to Him our cares, praise, and thanksgiving.

JESUS IN GETHSEMANE

Jesus is, of course, the best model for how we are to live, and this is true regarding prayer as well. Jesus was supernaturally minded. He lived before the face of God. This insight of God's presence saturated everything He saw, said, and touched. It is not the same for us in the West. Because of our culture's inherent rationalism, we must cultivate this kind of mindset. We have to work at it. We are inundated by naturalistic explanations of things, and so living before the face of God is difficult, and our sin deadens us to supernatural realities, something Jesus never experienced. Sin fogs and hardens us. This is the reason we need prayer. Prayer reorients us to this supernatural reality of things. It is a cultivation of our supernatural perception.

The disciples had this problem in Gethsemane the night before Jesus's death. They were warm with wine. They were tired. So, you might think they could be excused for falling asleep. You might say they are only human. But their Master had just told them to watch (Mark 14:34). He had also just told them that they would all betray Him by the time the sun came up the next morning (Mark 14:27). In the upper room, the Master had told them he was about to be betrayed and killed. All of this was to happen at any moment. Therefore, He called them to watch. To stay alert. To pray.

But Jesus came back to them three times and found them sleeping each time. How can we explain this? The explanation is more than merely wine and the fatigue of stress. It is a matter of weak flesh, an overestimation of their own strength in the face of impending conflict. They believed they were strong enough. They were industrious enough. Peter was going to draw his sword and take stabs at the enemy soldiers. He could rescue the Master out of the claws of death. He had it all figured out, and if he did not, he was witty and bold enough to find a way.

Whether in churches or in individuals, this is the problem of dead orthodoxy. In churches, dead orthodoxy thinks that because it has proper theology, expository preaching, a right administration of the sacraments, and healthy church discipline, everything else will take care of itself. Individually, we believe that because we have been baptized, attend church regularly, tithe, abstain from worldly lusts, and go through our Bible reading plan once a year, all is well.

All these things are good, just as Peter was indeed resourceful, brave, and a genuine lover of Jesus, evidenced by his repentance. But Jesus did not think that was enough. He told them to *watch and pray* (Mark 14:38). Their flesh was weak. They needed power from God. That is what prayer does. It stabilizes. It strengthens. It is an admission of weakness.

Now contrast Peter and the disciples with Jesus. He was also in Gethsemane. He had the same amount of wine and perhaps even less sleep, but He was more perceptive of His need of supernatural strengthening. He was *greatly distressed and troubled* (Mark 14:33). He said His soul was *very sorrowful, even to death* (Mark 14:34). He was being stretched to the limit. Luke told us, *His sweat became like great drops of blood falling down to the ground* (Luke 22:44), and the writer of Hebrews told us *Jesus offered up prayers and supplications, with loud cries and tears* (Hebrews 5:7). This horror of darkness was Jesus's awareness of what it meant for Him to drink the cup of God's wrath for sin the following day. He was to be made a propitiation, or one who turns away the righteous anger of God on behalf of His people. He was to be made a curse of the law, which was how sinners would be redeemed from that same curse (Galatians 3:13). He was to be made our substitute so that we, His sheep, could receive God's favor for eternity.

This is what drove Jesus to prayer. For Jesus, prayer was about being in God's presence. It was the wrestling of Jacob with God in solitude on the banks of the Jabbok River (Genesis 32:22). Prayer gave Jesus perspective of the issue at hand, especially in light of God's nature and presence. Prayer was a reminder that God is not just *God* but also our *Father*. He is not a tyrant but the One who bestows good gifts on His children, even if it means answering no to our prayers. That God is Father makes all the difference in the world for Jesus, knowing that when trials come, they come from a God who cares for us, even when we do not understand. Jesus rises from prayer calm, composed, resigned, and in charge. He gives a military command to "charge" or "advance," saying, *"Rise, let us be going; see, my betrayer is at hand"* (Mark 14:42). He walks toward the betrayer, not away from him.

GOD'S WILL IS TO BE FOREMOST

Jesus's agony in the garden reveals something else about prayer. Christ, aware of His impending sufferings, prayed that God would remove them. But this comes with a monumental caveat: suffering is removed only if it accords with God's will. Thus, the priority of prayer is always to be, *"Not my will, but yours, be done"* (Luke 22:42).

The Lord's Prayer teaches the same thing. Before we get to praying for *our daily bread,* Jesus told us to pray that God's *kingdom come* and His *will be done, on earth as it is in heaven* (Matthew 6:9-10). What does this mean? We must pray with God's kingdom in mind, not our own. James warned about praying with wrong motives, so that we may spend what we receive on our own pleasures (James 4:3). Still speaking of prayer, James went on to speak of friendship with the world as *enmity with God* (James 4:4). When our priorities are to advance our own kingdom, it is a type of friendship with the world.

In commenting on this petition of the Lord's Prayer, the "Westminster Shorter Catechism" exhorts us to "pray that God, by His grace, would make us able and willing to know, obey and submit to His will in all things, as the angels do in heaven."[53] This is why the aims of prayer matter. It is possible to be praying for the wrong thing, which in turn, puts us at risk of being enemies with God. It is the same for those with a dead orthodoxy. The aims of the prayers of those who have no vital

---

53   Westminster Shorter Catechism, Q&A 103.

union with God are bound to be earthward. Enlarge my bank account, my reputation, my success, and my kingdom. There is no sense of right priority. There is no sense of the glory of God.

The prayer of warm orthodoxy is different. It is not that we are to overlook our personal needs or consider them too unspiritual, but the heart of prayer should be *"Your kingdom come, your will be done."* The motive of prayer becomes putting God first: "Advance Your kingdom through me. If that means suffering, so be it. If that means being healed, so be it. If that means leaving destructive sins and patterns of behavior behind, so be it. Advance Your kingdom through my family, my church, my denomination. Do whatever it takes for this to happen. I am no longer my own. I have been bought with a price. I am a slave and soldier of the King of Kings. My life is to be about You, not me. I am utterly incapable of living entirely for You, but with your help, I can make great strides in this area. I thirst for this, and when I do not thirst for this, help my lack of thirst." This is the attitude of warm orthodoxy. The focus is God's glory, not my own.

THE STATE OF PRAYER TODAY

Yes, you say, but Christ's agony in the garden was an unusual time in the history of the church. No one has ever undergone the sufferings and torment that Christ went through on our behalf. It was right for Him to agonize in prayer over such a trial. Now that He has gone to the cross, died, and rose again, we can kick our feet up and wait for the results to organically unfold. There is no longer any great need to storm the throne room of God. It will all work itself out in the end.

Some of this is hyperbole, of course. Not many Christians would admit to such thinking. But our actions say otherwise. Our behavior reveals that this is how we view the situation. Our lives and churches are on autopilot. Our prayer lives are weak. Our prayer meetings are grossly unattended. Our prayers in church are unmemorable, dry, and without life. Our prayers before meals are quick and glib. Our prayers during family worship are without heat or tears. I do not want to accuse, but I do want to ask why this is so. Most of us would have to admit the above descriptions apply to us and our churches. We do not have well-attended prayer meetings, and we are not Christians whose knees are worn out from praying. Why are our prayers so often without life?

Indwelling sin is certainly an answer. Like the disciples, we, too, have weak flesh. We have consciences that accuse us. We have grudges and bitterness toward others. All of these things must be dealt with honestly and with repentance. Doing so will free us up to pray. Satan is another valid answer. We have an adversary, an opponent in the spiritual race of faith. The world, of course, is another factor. *The desires of the eyes and the pride of life,* or better translated *the pride of possessions,* makes us spiritually flabby (1 John 2:16). The drive for influence, success, and wealth can crowd out any time otherwise given to prayer. All of this is true. But that is exactly the point, is it not? Knowing we have such great obstacles should drive us to prayer, not away from it. Knowing how prone we are to dead orthodoxy should impel us to sit before the face of God as individuals, as churches, and as families, crying out for fresh measures of power and unction.

For instance, when Christ told the disciples to watch and pray, it applies to us as well. To *watch* means to "stay awake." Do not fall asleep. Sleeping is not much better than being dead. The Christian life should be anything but dead. Paul used the verbs *to run, press on, box, pull down strongholds, gird up your loins, fight the good fight, wage war,* and so on to describe the Christian life. He told the Ephesians to *look carefully then how you walk, not as unwise but as wise, making the best use of the time, because the days are evil* (Ephesians 5:15-16). Later, he said, *Be strong in the Lord and in the strength of his might. Put on the whole armor of God, that you may be able to stand against the schemes of the devil* (Ephesians 6:10-11).

Prayer is a non-negotiable practice for any Christian. It is the greatest act of faith because it necessitates that the person praying believes that God *is.* We are not merely uttering things into the void when we pray, but we are talking to God, to the God who hears and answers. We are not engaged in transcendental meditation when we pray. The point of prayer is not to evacuate the mind of all things, including "god," but rather to be intensely fixated on God and whatever it is we are praying about.

Every day the Christian faces trials, tests, and adversities. Christ said to not worry about tomorrow because *"sufficient for the day is its own trouble"* (Matthew 6:34). Every day the Christian is tempted to gossip, to be resentful, and to be proud. He is tempted to cheat on his taxes or spouse. He is tempted to be sluggish in the raising of his children. He is tempted to be sluggish at work. The world persecutes him for his faith. His lust for wealth and power tempts him to idolatrous practices and worship. In the church, the devil seeks to divide, deaden, and discourage the saints. Every day there are decisions to be made that tax and overwhelm the intellect: Where to send the kids to school? When to change jobs? Where to go to church? When to have that tough conversation with someone? What to buy at the grocery store? What not to buy? What to give money to? What not to give money to? When to share the gospel with the neighbor? Such demands require more prayer, not less. Such challenges require an orthodoxy that is alive and endued with power, not one that is dead or sleeping.

CORPORATE PRAYER

But prayer is not only an individual effort; we also see corporate prayer modeled in the Bible. In the Old Testament, we find the Israelites groaning, worshiping, singing, and praying together at regular intervals and especially in times of disaster or rejoicing. For example, Psalm 44 was written in the first-person plural, or *we*: *O God, we have heard with our ears, our fathers have told us, what deeds you performed in their days, in the days of old* (Psalm 44:1). Esther, Ezra, and Nehemiah all called for or led corporate prayers. In the New Testament, the data is just as rich. In the Lord's Prayer, Jesus told His disciples to pray, *"Our Father,"* not "my" Father. On the Day of Pentecost, the disciples were gathered in corporate prayer (Acts 2:42). On the night of Peter's release from jail, the church was praying together in the home of John Mark (Acts 12:12-17).

Corporate prayer meetings are times that are intentionally set apart for the purpose of praying as a church. There is no single right way to conduct a prayer meeting, but there are certainly many wrong ways to do it. For this reason, every prayer meeting should be prefaced with a few informal house rules. "Rules" and prayer meetings can seem like an anomaly, but God is a God of decency and order in prayer meetings too. And as you will see, such rules still allow for plenty of spontaneity.

First, because our lives are filled with distractions, business, frustrations, and dopamine blasts that can make settling into prayer difficult, begin the prayer meeting with a short and simple exhortation on the topic of prayer from the Scriptures. This will help foster an atmosphere in which prayer will thrive. When I say short, I mean five minutes, ten at the most. A prayer meeting should not be tacked onto the end of some other event such as a Bible study. Spurgeon wrote an entire book called *Only a Prayer Meeting*, which emphasized this point. Do not allow some other event or conversation to crowd out the prayer meeting. Also, the group may be inclined to converse or continue discussion about the exhortation well past the ten-minute mark. This is a very real temptation that the leader of the prayer meeting must patiently check. If we have an hour to pray and twenty minutes of it is taken up with discussion, the prayer meeting is cut almost in half. The purpose of the prayer meeting is to pray, not to talk about prayer – or anything else.

This is why the prayer meeting should not begin with prayer requests. This is a guaranteed way to kill a prayer meeting. We all know how this goes. It begins by asking people for prayer requests and then after they are shared aloud and commented on, the whole cycle happens again in the prayer. It is redundant and costs time. Because they have already heard the request, people may drift off and not be engaged in the prayer. Instead, in a prayer meeting, the people should simply pray their prayer requests.

This leads us to another point. It should be explained to the group that the focus of the corporate prayer meeting should be primarily about the church and other matters pertaining to the advance of the gospel on earth. It is often useful to have a list provided beforehand to help people better understand what is meant by this: the advance of the gospel to the nations; the building up of the local church; the comfort of the persecuted church; the increase of Christ's reign in our city; the vanquishing of the demonic and our foes; the rulers and magistrates who govern us; the ministers; and the sick and the poor. Specific needs within the church must be prayed for as well, including health concerns and even things that may appear less spiritual. Just because the focus should be on church-related matters does not mean these other needs should be disregarded or are somehow inferior. It is rather to say that the essence of the meeting should focus on the church, even though other pressing items should be prayed for as well.

We do not want to quench anyone's zeal, but an effective way to keep the prayer meeting moving is to limit the length of time for each prayer. A good rule of thumb is to pray for one petition at a time. Rather than one person spending ten to fifteen minutes praying through the list mentioned above, each person, in turn, should pray for one item on the list. This keeps the momentum moving along and prevents one person from taking up all the things to pray for. People can have more than one turn to pray, and there does not need to be a set order of who prays next. The group should pray as they are led, one person at a time, one petition at a time.

Generally, the meeting should be as spontaneous as possible. When things go silent for a while, the leader should remind the group that this is not a bad thing, as awkward as it may seem. Other times people will try to pray at the same time, but that too has a way of working itself out. The leader of the prayer meeting must work hard to instill these house rules while at the same time encouraging the group to relax and not overthink things.

The prayer meeting is the most important ministry or event in the church. It is more critical than evangelism, good preaching, robust fellowship, or good liturgy. This is because without the Holy Spirit blessing our evangelism, preaching, fellowship, the service, and every other component of the church plant, they will be done in the flesh. It will all unravel. Spurgeon noted, "At a certain meeting of ministers and church officers, one after another doubted the value of prayer meetings; all confessed that they had a very small attendance, and several acknowledged without the slightest compunction that they had quite given them up."[54] How can we expect souls to be saved if we have no genuine passion to pray for it to happen? How can we expect sin to be overcome if we are not petitioning God to this end?

---

54   Charles H. Spurgeon, "Another Word Concerning the Down-Grade," *The Sword and the Trowel* (August 1887), 397–98.

EXPECTANT PRAYER

Prayerlessness alone is not the problem. Most prayer meetings and prayer lives are marred by a droning unbelief. We do not expect to have our prayers answered. That is not the spirit of prayer that we see in the Scriptures. Even a casual study of prayer in the Bible will reveal that scriptural prayer is done in a spirit of boldness and expectation.

In Jesus's parable of the persistent friend, Jesus said it was the friend's *impudence* that finally got the other man out of bed to give him whatever he needed (Luke 11:8). The idea of praying with impudence is shocking, and it is even more shocking that it is Jesus who is saying this. If we saw things in their proper perspective, we would be going to God *without ceasing*, as Paul told us to do (1 Thessalonians 5:17). We would be doing this without any nudging from Jesus or anyone else. It would be instinctive. God is the author of life and the source of all power, wisdom, and beauty. We would be begging God to allow us to speak to Him and to give us such power. But in our sluggishness, we neglect this opportunity. We put it off or do not see the value of it. We might expect God to react to our negligence with vengeance or haughty distancing. "Fine, your loss," we would expect Him to say. But that is not what we find in the Scriptures. Not only are we repeatedly told to pray to God, but we are also told to do so with confidence and even impudence. He is the One who is pleading with us to pray to Him. What a marvelous wonder!

Paul told us that in Christ, we can have boldness and confidence before God (Ephesians 3:12). James told us to pray without doubting (James 1:6). John wrote, *And this is the confidence that we have toward him, that if we ask anything according to his will he hears us* (1 John 5:14). The author of Hebrews told us, *Let us then with confidence draw near to the throne of grace, that we may receive mercy and find grace to help in time of need*

(Hebrews 4:16). Jesus said, *"Therefore I tell you, whatever you ask in prayer, believe that you have received it, and it will be yours"* (Mark 11:24).

Matthew recorded Christ telling His disciples to keep on asking, knocking, and seeking whenever their prayers go unanswered (Matthew 7:7-12). Keep going. Do not quit. The parable of the unjust judge reinforces this (Luke 18:1-8). The judge did not fear God or care about the people, but there was a widow who persistently came to him seeking justice against her adversary. The judge eventually gave her justice because she kept bothering him. If that is true of this judge who neither feared God nor loved man, how much more will God be willing to answer the prayers of the persistent since God is righteous and told us to cast our anxieties on Him because He cares for us (1 Peter 5:7)?

These statements seem too good to be true. Dead orthodoxy will ask, Who are we to ask God expectantly? Who are we to presume God will answer our prayers? But in our attempts to be pious, we are being disobedient to the spirit in which God tells us to pray. We approach prayer with a wavering, unfaithful spirit. The praying we see in the Bible is bold, confident, and expectant.

Did Elijah pray with the kind of unbelief we so often find in ourselves? He prayed for a drought, and it happened. He prayed for rain, and it rained. Perhaps he didn't pray with the outward tears of Jesus in Gethsemane, yet his faith in God inspired him to pray fervently and with expectation. In the New Testament, James used Elijah as an example of what is expected from us all. This is why James said Elijah was a man like us, yet *the prayer of a righteous person has great power as it is working* (James 5:16).

Don't get me wrong. The "name it and claim it" gospel, otherwise known as the "prosperity gospel," is a perversion of what we see in the Scriptures. It does not sufficiently consider the sovereignty of God, and it often prioritizes man's will over God's will. But dead orthodoxy is at the other extreme, renouncing all expectation in the things we pray for, especially if they are prayers of healing, revival, conversion, church growth, or deliverance from significant sins. Dead orthodoxy is reluctant to pray for anything miraculous at all. We think that to do so would be tempting God. But we see the opposite in Scripture. To not pray with fervency and expectation is to tempt God. Is it any wonder then that dead orthodoxy does not see much in the way of revivals, miracles, church growth, or deliverance from sin? *You do not have, because you do not ask* (James 4:2).

WAKE-UP CALL

Dead orthodoxy does not just happen. It begins with us falling asleep and our prayer life deteriorating. Is our time in the Bible merely an exercise to get through? Are we even reading the Bible anymore? Have we stopped praying with fellow believers, confessing our sin, and giving our resentment to the Lord? Have we stopped going to church? Have sins such as lust, anger, bitterness, and sloth become overpowering?

These are all results of a diminished prayer life. When our souls begin to grow cold, our prayer lives are the first to suffer. We may still be involved in the church, in evangelism, in singing, in diaconal duties, but a shift has occurred. Something is going on in the soul as deadly as any rumbling of tectonic plates. A catastrophic earthquake is imminent. We fell asleep and stopped praying.

Our only hope is to wake up and call on the name of our God. The storms of sin, the devil, and the flesh are raging around us. Like Jonah, we are in danger of being overtaken by these monsters. Like the church in Sardis, we may have a reputation of being alive, but if our prayer life is non-existent, we are dead (Revelation 3:1). Jesus told this church: *"Wake up, and strengthen what remains and is about to die"* (Revelation 3:2). You have had seasons of sweet communion in the past, but now you feel dry and busy. Your faith has become nominal. When we find ourselves in the desert, call on God for rain. Look to Jesus for refreshment.

In great desperation, Judah's King Jehoshaphat cried out to God: *"O our God, will you not execute judgment on them? For we are powerless against this great horde that is coming against us. We do not know what to do, but our eyes are on you"* (2 Chronicles 20:12). What was God's response? He rescued him from all his troubles. Do we see our great need for God's power, His help, and His victory in our lives? Pray to Him. Call out to Him. Ask God to pour His Spirit on you again. Meet with Him in the closet of prayer. Repent, turn from the business of life, and sit with the Lord in the secrecy of His presence.

Without God moving on our ministry, neighborhood, family, nation, and even our own souls, no lasting spiritual work will get done. This is why we must plead with the Lord to move. When reading the Scriptures, we get the idea that urgent and persistent dealings with God are simply the normal routine of the Christian life. So, what has gone wrong in our own day? We greatly emphasize doctrine, study, exegesis, and theory but place little emphasis on prayer and spiritual disciplines.

My intent is not to weigh us down with a burden too heavy to bear, but rather to call things as they are and to urge us to confess and repent of this imbalance. Too often we intentionally stay busy instead of simply waiting on God in prayer. We will not put away our social media, television, and entertainment for the sake of shutting ourselves away in our closets, where our Father who sees us in secret will reward us openly (Matthew 6:6). *Wait for the* LORD; *be strong, and let your heart take courage;*

wait for the Lord! (Psalm 27:14). Go to Him and ask for help with this all-important task of prayer, believing that *the Lord is good; his steadfast love endures forever* (Psalm 100:5).

STUDY QUESTIONS

1. Would you describe your prayer life as strong or weak? Do you attend your church's prayer meetings?

2. What do you find most difficult about praying?

3. Do you pray with expectation, or do you feel like this would be tempting God?

4. Why do you think so many Christians have barren prayer lives? What are some possible remedies for this epidemic?

CHAPTER 8

SMUG CONTENTMENT

Christianity is unique among major world religions for its emphasis on doctrine and learning. Historically, when Christian missionaries go into a new place, one of the first things they do is start schools. Protestants, coming out of Roman Catholicism, believe it is especially important for each person to have a Bible and be able to read it. The intellect is crucial. This is why Christians are called "People of the Book." In Islam, simply memorizing the Koran is enough to obtain eternal life, even if you do not understand what you memorized. Not so with Christianity. John tells us that these things are written *so that you may believe that Jesus is the Christ, and that by believing you may have life in his name* (John 20:31). When reading the Bible, it is important to know what you are reading. It is important to know what the Bible teaches. This is not true only for Christian ministers. It is true for all Christians.

But as we have seen, the intellect is not the whole story. Intellect without the Holy Spirit is devastating. This is the idea of Paul's statement, *"Knowledge" puffs up* (1 Corinthians 8:1).

This leads us to our next phase of dead orthodoxy: *smug contentment*. Such an attitude is typically toxic and Machiavellian. It leads to tribalism, excessive criticism, and a condescending air toward others in general.

BIBLICAL CONTENTMENT VS. SMUG CONTENTMENT

Contentment is a good thing. Paul expresses as much in his letters: *I know how to be brought low, and I know how to abound. In any and every circumstance, I have learned the secret of facing plenty and hunger, abundance and need. I can do all things through him who strengthens me* (Philippians 4:12-13). Christian contentment is being able to resign ourselves to whatever circumstance we are in because of our trust in God. The carousel of external or internal fluctuations does not change our sense of the sufficiency found in Christ. That is Paul's idea of contentment.

But biblical contentment is not what I am speaking about here. I am addressing prideful contentment, the idea of smugness or excessive pride in ourselves, especially in our abilities or achievements. In dead orthodoxy, this smugness reveals itself in our pride of our doctrinal knowledge. No one is as smart as I am. I have nothing to learn, especially from those outside of my doctrinal camp.

We can also be smugly content in a sense of our own righteousness or piety in contrast to the sinners around us. We sneeringly wonder how could people act that way? How do they not know better? What is wrong with them? Perhaps most dangerously, it shows up in a type of apathy or nominalism that sees itself as above the demands of the gospel and the perils that come with the Christian life. I do not need the church, elders, the Word of God, sermons, or prayers. I am beyond all of that. I can make it without them. Those things are for less enlightened Christians.

Let's look more closely at doctrinal knowledge. We have noted that such knowledge is important, even imperative. One cannot be a Christian without right knowledge. But when wielded and bandied about without love, it becomes dangerous. The Pharisees were doctrinal precisionists, but they would not dare assume they may be wrong in their interpretation of certain things, especially about the Messiah. Surely the Messiah would not take time for prostitutes and tax collectors, would He? Doesn't He know who these sinners are? Surely, He would not take us to task for our extraneous view of Sabbath laws, dietary restrictions, and temple regulations, and He would certainly not be from Nazareth. Smugness described these Pharisees. They had a theological haughtiness that led to a disdain for others.

This is the point of Jesus's parable about the Pharisee and tax collector. *"The Pharisee, standing by himself, prayed thus: 'God, I thank you that I am not like other men, extortioners, unjust, adulterers, or even like this tax collector. I fast twice a week; I give tithes of all that I get'"* (Luke 18:11-12). His doctrinal knowledge had become poisonous. We could modify it for our times: "God, I thank you I am not like other men, dispensationalists, continuationists, street preachers, or even like this man who shouts 'Amen!' in the middle of service. I read Calvin twice a week. I do not talk to Arminians; I never get too emotional when preaching." In other words, I am content with my doctrinal knowledge. My worship is biblical, my Sabbath observance is impeccable, and my wife and children are submissive. I have arrived. There are no other groups outside of mine who have anything to teach me. There are no other Christians, especially the more immature ones, who could offer me anything of value. I am content. I am smug.

But Jesus tells us it is the other man, the ignorant sinner, who was justified. Notice the difference between his spirit and the theologically sound Pharisee: *"But the tax collector, standing far off, would not even lift up his eyes to heaven, but beat his breast, saying, 'God, be merciful to me, a sinner!'"* (Luke 18:13). Jesus is not interested here in doctrinal precision but in awareness of one's condition in the sight of God. Doctrinal precision is important. In fact, in one sense we could even say that the tax collector had doctrinal precision. He had a better awareness of God's holiness and his own sinfulness than the Pharisee did. But Jesus was pointing out the attitude of each man. One is smug and content. One is humble and repentant. The two attitudes could not be more disparate.

TRIBALISM

Smugness can lead to unhealthy forms of tribalism. In some ways, tribalism is inevitable. We all have our people we associate with, work with, and feel comfortable around. This is true in life and in the church. We all have "our tribe."

But there should not be any hostile, warlike kind of tribalism for Christians. For example, Christian denominations or associations of likeminded churches are good and even biblical. The New Testament assumes such connections among churches. There are numerous advantages to these, such as a sharing of resources, accountability, mutual encouragement, and a broader global and domestic reach with the gospel.

But does this mean our denomination or association is the only "Christian" group that exists? Is our church the only one that is faithful to the Scriptures? For example, is my camp, the conservative Presbyterians, the only legitimate expression of Christianity? We could narrow it down even more and say that it is not just conservative Presbyterians who are the only legitimate expression, but it is those who, like me, are classical postmillennialists who also believe in the perpetuity of the office of evangelist.

This is how tribalism becomes hyper-tribalism. I stop seeing my Second London Baptist brothers as just as much Christian as myself. This would be even more true when I consider Trinitarian Pentecostals or Arminian Southern Baptists. Because they do not hold to the five points of Calvinism, I begin to wonder if they are even saved. This is a kind of *doctrinal regeneration*. If your doctrine is not the same as mine, you are not a brother. Maybe a distant cousin, if that. James warned about these attitudes of partiality:

> *My brothers, show no partiality as you hold the faith in our Lord Jesus Christ, the Lord of glory. For if a man wearing a gold ring and fine clothing comes into your assembly, and a poor man in shabby clothing also comes in, and if you pay attention to the one who wears the fine clothing and say, "You sit here in a good place," while you say to the poor man, "You stand over there," or, "Sit down at my feet," have you not then made distinctions among yourselves and become judges with evil thoughts?* (James 2:1-4)

There are expressions of Christianity more legitimate than others, and we should be seeking to conform more and more to a correct expression, whatever it may be. Inevitably, some groups are closer to that goal than others, and discussing and even debating what the goal is can be useful and proper. I am not advocating for some kind of generic unity among Christians. We should contend for the faith, including ecclesiology and doctrine. There will always exist differences among groups and even differences within each group. That is not in question here. What we need to answer is how we see professing Christians who are not part of our camp. Do we consider them lesser brothers than ourselves? Weaker? Dumber? Are we condescending in our attitudes toward them? Here is a way to test this: Do you pray for the church down the road, or do you see them as the competition? When you do pray for them, do you do so as co-heirs in the kingdom or as the superior brother praying for the lesser?

This tribalistic mindset generates serious problems within the local church, as well. If we are tribalistic toward those outside our camp or denomination, what happens when people from that camp come to church with us? What happens when someone who has been listening to prosperity preachers for the last five years comes into our church? Or someone whom God saved under the ministry of Jimmy Swaggert or Billy Graham? Or the hyper-dispensational who has just moved into the area and is checking out churches? What about the guy who just got out of prison and whose doctrine is a mess but is hungry to be around other believers? What about the blue-haired feminist with a nose ring and neck tattoos but who was given a gospel tract and wants to know more about the Lord? Will we be able to warmly welcome them and converse with them without condescension?

This is often a problem in churches that pride themselves on proper doctrine. Usually, when a person is converted, they come with bad doctrine. At the very least, it is influenced by whatever they were exposed to before they were a Christian, and for most people living in the West, it means something less than robust. These doctrinal churches want to grow, but growth assumes that many doctrinally immature and even unsound people are going to be attaching themselves to the church. Are you okay with this? How will tribalistic people respond to these immature seekers and new believers? Will they be patient with them? Will they walk alongside them without condescension or arrogance? Will they look down on them?

What if these new people show some resistance to accepting the church's doctrine? They are not exactly recalcitrant, but they are not quite ready to fully commit, or perhaps they still need more understanding. Will the church show them the door, or does it spend time discipling them, even if it takes years? Paul says, *In humility count others more significant than yourselves* (Philippians 2:3). The proud and smug are willing to count others more significant only after they achieve a certain level of doctrinal knowledge, and not before. There is an expectation that the new Christian should be at the same level as the veteran, and if not, he is not worth socializing with or helping.

This was the attitude of the Pharisees toward those they perceived as doctrinally immature. When Jesus healed the man born blind, the Pharisees pounced on him. Who was it who healed you? What are your thoughts about Him? What did He say to you? The healed man reservedly said that the Man is a prophet. But they did not accept such an answer. They pounced again. *"We know that this man is a sinner,"* they told him (John 9:24). This would mean that the Man is not a prophet. He is not from God, and He did not do this miracle. But the healed man insisted otherwise, until finally, exasperated, the Pharisees answered: *"You were born in utter sin, and would you teach us?" And they cast him out* (John 9:34). The Pharisees believed the doctrinally ignorant had nothing to teach them. This is smug contentment. This is dead orthodoxy.

Often, those who are immature in doctrine are more mature than others in Christian living, zeal, love, and humility. We can see this in some churches whose theology is light at best. They are not experts in Calvin or the Reformation, but they love their Bibles, Jesus, and their neighbors. They love the convict and the prostitute. Say what we want about such doctrinally-thin churches, they seem to get the part about *consider others more significant than yourselves* much better than some doctrinally sound churches do. Maturity is more than having doctrinal knowledge.

This was why even Jesus came under heavy scrutiny from the Pharisees. He was "unlearned." He was from Galilee, which was backwoods country. Anyone from Galilee would have been considered less reputable in matters of theology and religion than those from the south, where Jerusalem was. That Jesus came from there, without any education to speak of, would have been automatically disqualifying. There was nothing to learn from such a man. We do the same thing when it comes to those outside of our doctrinal camps. If they are not aligned with our view of things, they are not worth learning from, which is an indirect way of questioning whether they are even Christians like we are.

The disciples themselves thought this way on at least one occasion. The apostle John told Jesus, *"We saw someone casting out demons in your name, and we tried to stop him, because he was not following us"* (Mark 9:38). Another way to phrase it could be, "We tried to stop him, because he was not a Calvinist." Or if you are not a Calvinist, you could say, "because he was a Calvinist."

The point is that they assumed the only true Christians out there were the little band who were with them. Anyone who was not part of their group was to be stopped. The fact that John reported their behavior to Jesus makes us assume that he believed Jesus would congratulate him for such a thing, but He does not: *But Jesus said, "Do not stop him, for no one who does a mighty work in my name will be able soon afterward to speak evil of me. For the one who is not against us is for us"* (Mark 9:39-40). How often have we fallen into the same trap? How often have we thought that only our group is being faithful to the gospel and that other groups out there, even those faithful to the five solas, for instance, are to be either stopped or looked down on?

WILD HORSES DRAGGING ME AWAY

As an undergraduate student reading through the Bible, I still remember my surprise to find that God's people are expected to be meek, gentle, kind, humble, and patient, among other things. This may seem silly to some readers, but for a blue-collar young man from rural New Mexico who was used to fighting, cussing, spitting, and partying, it was shocking. This was no easy task. It is now more obvious than ever how necessary the Holy Spirit is for bringing about such fruit. Who else could do it? Even more surprising was that I wanted to pursue such a life, which was foreign and even antithetical to the culture I was used to. This is not to say I mastered it then or now, but the passion for it was there, and it continues to be true to this day in varying degrees. This can be attributed to none other than the Spirit of God.

Scripture's overwhelming emphasis on the pursuit of purity and holiness is a far cry from the fire-breathing war cries too often heard in Christian churches, circles, and especially on social media today. It is certainly very different from the volcano of passion that was steadily streaming from my own heart anytime I got a whiff of sin, doctrinal inconsistency, or a spiritual life that was less than robust. When I entered ministry, my attitude became even worse. I was on fire for the Lord but was outraged when others were not, especially pastors or longtime Christians. I became impatient and proud. What is wrong with other people? Why can't they see it like I do? Shouldn't those people know better?

I was also surprised to see in the Scriptures an emphasis on unity, peace among the body, love, and forbearance. This struck me with a firm and stinging hand. These truths have been further confirmed over the years but so has my understanding of how difficult such things are to achieve. Meekness, gentleness, and patience often seem like a faraway dream. Unity and forbearance among Christians seem like something reserved only for glory. This is no excuse for negligence or carnality. Rather, it is even more reason to look earnestly to Christ, pleading for more outpourings of the Spirit.

What I learned was that there is a Christianity that is hard, dry, and strident. And there is its contrast, which we see exemplified in the life of Jesus and written about in the letters of the New Testament. It finds ample space in the Old Testament as well, especially in the lives of Moses, David, and kings such as Josiah. There is a spirit from above and another one from below. There is a time and place for the Christian to dispute, fight, defend, contend, and charge ahead, but there is also a right spirit in which to do it. Much of dead orthodoxy is simply a case of pursuing the Christian life with the wrong spirit. I acknowledge this with grief in my heart, admitting my own failings in this area in the past. But I also acknowledge it with joy, knowing that admission of the problem is essential for recovery.

While pastoring on the Navajo Reservation, I frequently would see mustangs stampeding up and down the streets. These creatures were fierce, lovely, confident, bold as lions, and surprisingly useless. Many Christians today are like those mustangs. We can be militant in our zeal, we can be brash, and we can fight all the legions of unbelief, feminism, culture, and sin with bared teeth, manes flowing, and hoofs spraying sparks. But in our recklessness, we destroy everything in sight. We trample down anyone and anything in our way. We pulverize bruised reeds and douse the smoking flax (Matthew 12:20). We are angry and rough. I had that attitude years ago, and it continues to be a threat when not checked by the Spirit of God or faithful men in my life.

This leads us to the biblical idea of *meekness*. It is not a relinquishing of prowess or zeal but the humble and gracious use of it. It is the harnessing of such strength for the purpose of pleasing God and serving our neighbor. It conveys the idea of tameness and often comes through brokenness and humility. It is the Spirit of God leading the human spirit. This is the yoke Christ calls us to and the school from which He expects us to learn. This is the secret between an orthodoxy that is alive and one that is dead. Broken mustangs make the best horses. They still have buck, but it is channeled in the right direction. They are warm, sweet, and tender but still bold, fierce, and flowing. This is also true of all Christians who are living in the power of the Holy Spirit.

SPIRIT VS. LETTER

Jesus told the Pharisees that He was looking for mercy, not sacrifice. If they had known what that meant, they *"would not have condemned the guiltless"* (Matthew 12:7). Jesus rebuked them because they were concerned only for the law, not the spirit of the law. That is often true of us. We are so concerned about doctrinal precision that we lose the warmth, tenderness, and genuine affection that our doctrine should be producing within us. When I see myself or my tribe as the only genuine exponents of the Christian religion, it undermines the universal nature of the Christian religion.

Yes, doctrine is important, and there are Christians and camps within Christianity that may be closer to right doctrine than others. That is inevitable. But there are also Christians and camps within Christianity who are closer to right orthopraxy, or right Christian living, than others. What about them? Should they not be able to teach us? The ideal state would be a fusion of both right doctrine and right orthopraxy, but because of limitations caused by the flesh and immaturity, both doctrinally and practically, this is elusive. Thus, it is wise to accept that others outside your tribe are also genuine Christians and can faithfully put forward true articulations of faith and practice.

Of course, we should not allow heresy. There are false expressions of Christianity, such as Jehovah's Witness, Roman Catholicism, and Mormonism. We should not tolerate these teachings, but in what spirit should we approach Mormons and Jehovah's Witnesses? Do we see them as beneath us, or do we recognize that but for the grace of God we, too, would be what they are, believe what they believe, and follow what they follow? The same is true of doctrinal errors. People who hold such errors are deceived, but who can open their eyes to this fact? God does, yes, but He typically uses brothers and sisters who come alongside them in a spirit of love and patience, not elitism or smugness, and over time, they are often corrected or rescued. There is a time to not throw pearls to swine, particularly if a person is unteachable, but often, our own doctrinal elitism is what keeps us from committing to people entangled in error. We think there is no hope for them. We think they should know better, so it would not be worth the effort to walk alongside them through this process. They are not worth our time. This is tribalism at its worst. My camp keeps company with my camp and no one else. I can only learn from my kind of people and no one else. The other camps do the same. When we do get together, it is to belittle and argue, not to patiently work together in a spirit of love for the sake of coming to a better understanding of what the Scriptures teach.

Is this not what Paul was condemning in the Corinthian churches? *For when one says, "I follow Paul," and another, "I follow Apollos," are you not being merely human? What then is Apollos? What is Paul?"* (1 Corinthians 3:4-5). Apollos and Paul were not the same person. They would have emphasized different things. They would have been passionate about different things. These differences in emphasis and personality led to the formation of different camps, but Paul told the Corinthians that such tribalism was improper.

The same is even more true regarding personality differences. We all know how easy it is to gravitate to one person over another because of personality. This is true also of certain churches and denominations. Two churches may have the same doctrine yet a completely different culture. Does that mean one is superior to the other or that one is Christian and the other not? Not necessarily, and that was Paul's point here. Both Apollos and Paul were servants of the Lord. One would be stronger in some areas than the other, and vice versa, but they were both the Lord's. They were both *servants through whom you believed* (1 Corinthians 3:5), but it is God who gave the growth (1 Corinthians 3:6). Some Christians, churches, and denominations will be stronger in some areas than others, but no one church or denomination is the only true expression. The church is the instrument through which people are edified in the faith and the gospel spread to the nations. Tribalism is to some extent inevitable, but the elitist, condescending, and strident type is never justified. This is what it means to be *of the flesh and behaving only in a human way* (1 Corinthians 3:3).

Isn't it ironic that when revival comes to an area, unity increases among the different denominations? That harmony exists among groups that have before been at odds? And at the same time, that when disunity appears, the revival seems to wane? Or is it perhaps that the disunity reemerges because of this waning of God's Spirit? That is what church history shows. The logical conclusion is that a warm, living orthodoxy rubs away the edges of tribalism, while dead orthodoxy hardens and defines them.

Are we jealous of another church that is outgrowing ours or another servant who is more influential than we are? Are we embittered toward Christians because they differ with us in matters of non-essential doctrine? If I am a premillennial, do I look condescendingly on postmillennials? What about the reverse? Doctrine is not irrelevant, even in matters of eschatology, but we need to ask what our heart is like toward Christians who are not in our camp. Do we struggle to get along with other camps? Are there tribes we resent? Do we scour the internet and social media headhunting for anyone who offers a view that differs from our own? Do we do the same thing in our churches or even our families?

There is a fine line between contending for the faith and being hypercritical, and we need to evaluate our hearts and behavior to assess where it is we have crossed that line. I think every Christian has done so at some point or another, so there is nothing to deflect, defend, or avoid here. We need to confess, repent, and go back to our brothers and sisters with a humble and contrite heart, even in matters of disagreement. We need discernment to know when to attack, so to speak, and when to hold our tongue or approach the issue with a different, more patient tone.

THE CRITICAL SPIRIT

There are two types of critical spirit. One is self-critical, which is the type that we saw in the tax collector. This spirit excels at introspection and lamentation. Taking it to its extreme could lead to despondency and a lack of assurance. Such a spirit should be counseled to keep looking to Jesus, the author and finisher of our faith, resting in His finished work alone for salvation and favor in the eyes of God. This person may have a tendency toward perfectionism, which in turn leads to guilt, frustration, and self-esteem issues. This kind is not our main concern in this book, although there may be a link between this type of critical spirit and the other one.

In dead orthodoxy, there appears a spirit of criticism that is more external in its focus. Rather than the self-absorbed kind of critic, this one will be concerned with the shortcomings of other people, churches, and denominations. It, too, has a perfectionist mindset but mainly when it concerns others. It is prone to constant complaining or murmuring.

Surprisingly, the Bible has quite a lot to say about a murmuring spirit. It is certainly an underappreciated topic in the evangelical world, perhaps because we are all so prone to do it. James said, *Do not grumble against one another* (James 5:9). Peter told believers to *show hospitality to one another without grumbling* (1 Peter 4:9). Jude described the false teachers as *grumblers, malcontents, following their own sinful desires* (Jude 1:16). The strongest warning came from Paul. He pointed out that the Israelites in the wilderness were destroyed by the angel of death for grumbling (1 Corinthians 10:9-10).

Why is a critical spirit a mark of dead orthodoxy? Because it stems from a deficient view of the gospel and a lack of contentment and love. As humans, we are naturally prone to sin. We are fickle and unreliable. We are self-centered and limited in our understanding, wisdom, and affection for others. This is not a justification for these things but is merely the truth. Unfortunately, this remains true of us even after we become Christians. Although there is a true change and growth in Christ, our old man still hampers us far too often. But this is exactly what makes the gospel so astounding. It is precisely for people like us that God sent forth His Son to die. He came to redeem God-haters from their sin. He came to make us into new creations with new minds, new affections, and new desires. He continues to intercede for us, despite our continual shortcomings and sin.

A critical spirit does not assess people in this light. We have seen that dead orthodoxy can lead to a spirit of elitism, where only my group is correct and everyone else is beneath me, and this leads to a critical spirit. If I am constantly critical of other people's behavior, I have not yet come to grips with the fact that Christ loved such people and has been immensely patient with them, especially those who are Christians, and He calls me to be so as well. A critical spirit is too dismissive of the grace and kindness that God bestows on people, including the one with the critical spirit, every day.

This is why Paul told the Ephesian church: *Let all bitterness and wrath and anger and clamor and slander be put away from you, along with all malice. Be kind to one another, tenderhearted, forgiving one another, as God in Christ forgave you* (Ephesians 4:31-32). Paul encouraged the believers to have a non-critical spirit. This is a spirit that the gospel has tenderized and humbled. It is a spirit that considers *others more significant* than themselves (Philippians 2:3).

The disciples exhibited this attitude at the Last Supper on the night Jesus was betrayed. Jesus told them that one of them would betray Him. Dead orthodoxy's response would be, "Is it he?" There would be finger pointing and silent accusations. But the disciples amazingly ask, *"Is it I?"* (Mark 14:19). They are humble enough to point the finger in their own direction first because they have become acquainted with their own shortcomings and need for grace.

This is an orthodoxy that is living, not dead. It is an attitude Paul expected all the churches to have. As critical as right doctrine is, Paul emphasized love toward each other and unity among believers – even when people or circumstances makes it difficult. A hypercritical spirit does the opposite. It is divisive and Pharisaical. If God had such a spirit toward us, where would we be?

WHAT TO DO ABOUT SMUGNESS

Like many aspects of dead orthodoxy, smugness, theological elitism, and a critical spirit are caused by pride. Once detected in our own hearts, repentance would include humbling ourselves and calling out to God from a broken and contrite spirit. Jesus had this in mind when He said, *"Whoever humbles himself like this child is the greatest in the kingdom of heaven"* (Matthew 18:4). In an earlier chapter, we saw that Jesus thanked the Father that He had hidden gospel truths *from the wise and understanding and revealed them to little children* (Matthew 11:25). The word *children* here is a metaphor for humility and spiritual simplicity. Educationally speaking, Jesus's first disciples were not of the caliber of the Pharisees. They were not educated in the Law as the Pharisees were, but in another sense, they would far surpass them in the actual teachings of the Law.

The same is true today. We may have doctrinal precision. We may have memorized the historic creeds and confessions of the church and be familiar with all the nuances of classical or presuppositional apologetics. But do we have love? Do we have warmth for our neighbors who do not know as much as we do? Do we have tenderness, even toward our enemies?

Augustine of Hippo said that the precepts or chief rules of the Christian religion are first, humility; second, humility; and third, humility.[55] He did not think prayer was the foremost Christian precept. Nor did he think it was fasting, preaching, or giving alms. He said humility is the most important virtue of Christianity. The reason for this is simple. Without humility, what would fasting, preaching, or alms do? What is

---

55   Calvin, *Institutes*, 2.2.10.

correct doctrine without humility? Fasting and praying without humility would do more harm than good, as would prideful preaching or prideful giving of alms. This is why Augustine called humility the foundation of the Christian religion. It is that on which everything else is built.

So how do we fan the flames of humility and love, especially for those we have difficulty loving? We can start by praying for them. Jesus prescribed this formula in the Sermon on the Mount: *"But I say to you, Love your enemies and pray for those who persecute you, so that you may be sons of your Father who is in heaven. For He makes His sun rise on the evil and on the good, and sends rain on the just and on the unjust"* (Matthew 5:44-45).

We may not think of our more immature or difficult brothers as enemies, but our condescension and irritability toward them are the same ingredients that foster an environment of enmity. Praying for them is the medicine given to us by Jesus. We should not pray for them to get smarter or to become as good as we are. That is pride. And we should not complain about them to God. We should, through prayer, genuinely seek their good. As we spend time sincerely praying for them, our soul's affection and tenderness will increase toward them.

The other remedy is to consider ourselves in light of the gospel. Who are we to complain about the faults of another? We have enough faults of our own, yet how does God treat us? He welcomes us, He loves us, and He considers us co-heirs with His Son.

WHAT ABOUT THE RELIGIONISTS?

I have directed much of this chapter at those who are smug and proud in their orthodoxy. But what about those of us who are sincerely aiming at warm orthodoxy? In our zeal to go Pharisee hunting, are we Pharisees ourselves? In our pursuit of snuffing out smugness, have we become smug and bitter toward the religionists and formalists? To be honest, that is the most difficult part of writing or even reading a book such as this one. It is easy to criticize those people, but in doing so, have we taken on a critical spirit? *Brothers, if anyone is caught in any transgression, you who are spiritual should restore him in a spirit of gentleness. Keep watch on yourself, lest you too be tempted* (Galatians 6:1).

Turn with me again to Paul. As we have seen, he was anything but a religionist. His orthodoxy was far from dead. If anyone had an excuse to rail against dead orthodoxy and smugness, it was Paul. He had left such a camp only to be actively hunted and persecuted by it. But what was his response? How did he speak about these people caught up in dead religion?

> *I am speaking the truth in Christ – I am not lying; my conscience bears me witness in the Holy Spirit – that I have great sorrow and unceasing anguish in my heart. For I could wish that I myself were accursed and cut off from Christ for the sake of my brothers, my kinsmen according to the flesh. They are Israelites, and to them belong the adoption, the glory, the covenants, the giving of the law, the worship, and the promises. To them belong the patriarchs, and from their race, according to the flesh, is the Christ, who is God over all, blessed forever. Amen.* (Romans 9:1-5)

Notice the passion in this man. When is the last time we had *great sorrow and unceasing anguish* in our hearts over those in our orbit caught up in dead orthodoxy? Isn't our typical reaction to be hard and sharp with them, the same thing we do not like about dead orthodoxy? Could we honestly wish we were *accursed and cut off from Christ* for the sake of those ensnared by cold religiosity?

Whether you are a smug formalist or a pursuer of true, warm orthodoxy, there is room for repentance on both sides. There is room in the kingdom of heaven for both Jews and Gentiles, religionists and fanatics, but only through the blood of Jesus. *For as in one body we have many members, and the members do not all have the same function, so we, though many, are one body in Christ, and individually members one of another* (Romans 12:5). Each of us is in a different stage of sanctification. That means our knowledge of doctrine is in varying stages as well. Those with a warm orthodoxy are patient toward others and humble regarding how they view themselves. Warm orthodoxy will *bear one another's burdens, and so fulfill the law of Christ. For if anyone thinks he is something, when he is nothing, he deceives himself* (Galatians 6:2-3). So whichever side of the orthodoxy spectrum you find yourself on, bow before the Maker in humble adoration, knowing that it is the gospel alone that qualifies us as worthy in His sight.

STUDY QUESTIONS

1. What is your tribe? Where do you feel comfortable? Be as specific as possible.

2. How do you view those who are not of your tribe?

3. Give an example of a time you have worked or fellow-shipped with people outside your tribe? What was your experience?

4. Have others from outside of your tribe ever treated you as inferior or ignorant because you were not part of their group? How did it make you feel?

CHAPTER 9

PRAGMATISM

You may think that because dead orthodoxy is *dead*, an orthodoxy that is living will be energetic and full of zest, charisma, and noise. It will have the bounce and shine of television preachers. It will have music that rivals Metallica and *American Idol*. Its evangelism will be all smiles, water bottles, and copious amounts of the sinner's prayer.

But that would be exchanging one type of dead orthodoxy for another. There is a dead orthodoxy that is dry, wooden, hypercritical, and often sectarian and elitist, but there is another type of dead orthodoxy that is just as counterfeit, if not more so. It is the kind that is never critical or serious about sin. It is never offensive, always upbeat, and squeamishly positive. It preaches from a bar stool and its members worship amidst smoke machines and colored lights. And it is thoroughly immersed in pragmatism.

THE PROBLEM WITH PRAGMATISM

We have seen throughout this book that because dead orthodoxy is dead, it needs to latch on to other things to make up for its deadness. It needs to manufacture the energy, liveliness, power, and zeal of a living orthodoxy. But pragmatism comes in many shapes and sizes. It can be Easter egg drops at a Sunday morning service or squishy, non-confrontational sermons. It can be dished out through an excessive diet of secondary topics at church, such as political theory, manliness, and eschatological topics like prophecy, dominion, and the end of the world. These topics are often chosen and conducted not for the sake of edification, which is one thing, but for getting people in the door. Those in charge know this kind of stuff sells, so they dole it out to the masses.

Pragmatism is the idea that the value or worth of a thing is determined by the results it produces. In Christianity, it means that if a method or style or topic works to attract people, it is more valuable than a method or style that does not, regardless of what the Bible says about it. If it works, do it. Pragmatism is the result of not having the power of God, so alternative methods or practices are needed to make up for it. This is why it is an element of dead orthodoxy.

This may seem surprising since many churches that would not consider themselves dead, such as charismatic ones, often deploy pragmatism more than others. That is because the aim of those churches is typically numerical success, even if it is counterfeit. Revival, evangelism, and church growth become a marketing challenge. This approach has caused a downgrade in Western Christianity seen as far back as the nineteenth century when New York pastor James Alexander said: "The gospel is not attractive enough for people now-a-days. Ministers must bait their trap with something else. The old-fashioned topics are seldom heard."[56]

---

56   Iain Murray, *Revival & Revivalism*, (Carlisle, PA: Banner of Truth, 1994), 337.

Iain Murray has stated that this pragmatic approach is why the church's *true authority and strength* was eventually sapped in the 1800s: "In the end, while evangelicalism was seeking to guard faith in Scripture, it was her readiness to be impressed by pragmatic arguments, and by alleged success, by quantity rather than quality, that did so much to deprive her of true authority and strength."[57] We are told by a firsthand witness that the same thing plagued the Welsh Revival of 1904-05: "So great was the passion for results that men forgot what was due to reverence and even to decency. . . . It is possible to sacrifice too much for the sake of results, and such results are seldom enduring."[58]

WHAT ABOUT HELL?

Consider the topic of hell as a case study. Why is hell downplayed in many circles today? Why is there an unspoken belief that we must tone down all mention of hell or future judgment when talking to the lost, otherwise they will walk away from the gospel? Why is there a reluctance to preach on hell or other hard topics in church? Why are we reluctant to bring it up in our conversations with the lost? Why do we speak of "scaring people into heaven" pejoratively, as if believing in Jesus to avoid hell is a bad motive? Jesus Himself said, *"Unless you repent, you will all likewise perish"* (Luke 13:3). He said elsewhere, *"For it is better that you lose one of your members than that your whole body go into hell"* (Matthew 5:30). It seems Jesus thought that speaking of hell as an inducement for becoming His disciple was a perfectly valid thing to do. It is common sense to want to avoid hell, yet there seems to be a reluctance to say these things in much of the church today.

---

57   Ibid., 383.
58   J. Vyrnwy Morgan, *The Welsh Religious Revival, 1904–5: A Retrospect and a Criticism* (London: Chapman & Hall, 1909), 140.

For instance, formally, many Christians would say they believe in hell, but how many would say that to speak much of hell is an ineffective, if not harmful, approach? The term *fire and brimstone* is used today in a pejorative sense, even by Christians, even though two centuries ago it was a common topic of preaching, whether in church or to the lost. There is a tacit belief that preaching on hell and judgment does not work in a culture as sophisticated as ours. But Tertullian, who wrote around AD 200, showed that the same ridicule and scorn regarding hell was cast on Christians in his day too: "We get ourselves laughed at for proclaiming that God will one day judge the world, though, like us, poets and philosophers set up a judgment seat in the world below. And if we threaten Gehenna, a reservoir of secret fire under the earth for purposes of punishment, we have derision heaped upon us."[59]

This implies that the Christians were speaking about hell in their evangelism, despite the derision heaped upon them by the culture. And nowhere in the writings of the early church is there any mention of Christians recommending a more soft-pedaled approach to topics such as hell to accommodate such a sophisticated culture as theirs. We read nothing about Christians arguing that people in their day were different than those in the Old Testament times, so the church should implement another strategy. But unlike the early church, the modern church has an obsession for pragmatics. Because we do not have the Holy Spirit's power, we must come up with a clever, inoffensive way to present the gospel.

We can see this same reality in popular TV shows such as *The Chosen*. Because the church is so deprived of power and unction, we think we must water down the gospel and make it more palatable for the masses. It is an attempt to make up for our dead orthodoxy by painting Christianity in attractive colors.

59   Tertullian, "Apology," *The Ante-Nicene Fathers*, ed. Alexander Roberts and James Donaldson (Peabody, MA: Hendrickson, 1994), 47.

As we saw above, Paul had the opposite view. He believed the power of the gospel was in its unattractiveness.

HYPER-CONTEXTUALIZATION: ALL THINGS TO ALL PEOPLE

Paul's comment on being *all things to all people* (1 Corinthians 9:19-23) is worth looking at from a slightly different angle than the one presented in an earlier chapter since this phrase has been the most popular target of hyper-contextualization.

Hyper-contextualization is not the same thing as *contextualization*. The idea of contextualization is a necessary one for any Christian. It simply means that we live and operate in a certain context, and we need to be aware of such a context in order to effectively communicate the gospel to the people living there. A rural context is different from an urban one. Your family gathering at Christmas is a different context than the one at work. Contextualization would include activities like preaching in Spanish when in Mexico and the idea of not offending cultural norms in the Middle East. Those ideas are consistent with what Paul had in mind. If it means being alert to the nuances and distinctives in an area in which you are ministering, it is absolutely biblical. But this is not what people usually mean when they use contextualization in contemporary conversations.

The idea of context has been prone to pragmatic abuse. Tertullian, for instance, talked about Christians in his own day using Paul's words to justify idolatry or attendance at heathen rituals. He responded to such hyper-contextualization by saying, "Of course he [God] does not so slacken those reins of conversations that, since it is necessary for us both to live and mingle with sinners, we may be able to sin with them too."[60] Calvin, who was also aware of people abusing Paul's words,

---

60 Tertullian, "On Idolatry," *The Ante-Nicene Fathers*, ed. Alexander Roberts and James Donaldson (Peabody, MA: Hendrickson, 1994), 69.

wrote: "Those who do not distinguish between things which are neutral and things which are forbidden are doubly in the wrong. Because they do not make that distinction, they have no hesitation about undertaking things which God has forbidden in order to please men. But their crowning sin is their making wrong use of this sentence of Paul's to make excuses for their own wicked hypocrisy."[61]

I call what they mean hyper-contextualization. Hyper-contextualization is allowing the world to set the agenda for how we evangelize or plant churches. Since the world likes amusement, we should include amusement in our presentation of the gospel. If we are evangelizing at a college campus, we should try to entice them with college-age activities like foosball, video games, or an occasional beer. If we are evangelizing a group of bikers, we should wear a biker's vest and use biker lingo. Better yet, we should buy a Harley-Davidson. The world is attracted to ballets, especially in cosmopolitan New York City, so we should have ballets during our worship services. The world likes skits and humor, so we should use them to break the ice before sharing the gospel with the lost. The idea is that making ourselves and the message more attractive to unbelievers will in turn draw them to believe the gospel.

This is not to say we should be insensitive to differences among groups, such as bikers in Idaho versus businessmen in New York City. Foosball with a college student would not be a compromise of the gospel. In fact, it is wise to try to explain things in symbols and language that the person or group you are dealing with would understand. But that is contextualization, not hyper-contextualization, or pragmatism. Hyper-contextualization or pragmatism is the idea that I have to embrace and promote worldly activities, theories, or culture in order for the gospel to attract people. For the gospel to be

---

61   John Calvin, *The First Epistle of Paul to the Corinthians*, trans. John W. Fraser (Grand Rapids, MI: Eerdmans, 1960), 196.

effective in contexts such as biker gangs or downtown New York City, it has to be tailored and warped to fit in with that crowd. If it is not, then it will not work.

Paul called for something completely different. As we have seen, Paul is a soul winner, but he pointed out that he has deliberately denied himself certain liberties in order to be a more effective soul winner. This passage in 1 Corinthians is about running and winning in matters of evangelism (1 Corinthians 9:24-26). It is about being a qualified evangelist whom God used to bring the gospel to the lost. It is about having a goal and rules when sharing the gospel. It is not about acting, dressing, or speaking like the world to attract the world to the gospel. It is not about hiding the gospel behind entertainment and humor or establishing common ground with the hearers until they are ready to receive the message of the gospel. "Current church growth methodology claims that if an evangelist wants to 'reach the culture' (whatever that means), he must emulate the culture in some way. But such an approach runs contrary to the biblical paradigm."[62]

William Carey provided a good illustration of Paul's meaning. One of the agreements that Carey and his colleagues came up with while serving as missionaries in India was to avoid offending non-Christians by their mannerisms: "Those parts of English manners which are most offensive to them [the Indians] should be kept out of sight as much as possible."[63] It does not mean he was going to indulge in cultural extravagances for the sake of making the gospel more attractive to the world, whether it be meat offered to idols or a game of beer pong at a college party. Far from acting like the world for the sake of attracting them to the gospel, Paul spoke about giving up certain liberties that might be offensive.

---

62   John MacArthur, "Theology of Sleep," in *Evangelism* (Nashville: Thomas Nelson, 2011), 3.

63   "The Serampore 'Form of Agreement' (1805)," *Wholesome Words Home*, accessed February 21, 2019, www.wholesomewords.org/missions/bcarey13.html.

Peter had the same view when writing to the churches in Pontus, Galatia, Cappadocia, Asia, and Bithynia, reminding them to *conduct yourselves with fear* during the time of their stay on earth (1 Peter 1:17) and that they had been called *out of darkness into his marvelous light* for the purpose of proclaiming *the excellencies of him* (1 Peter 2:9). Peter reminded them a couple verses later that they are *sojourners and exiles* in the world (1 Peter 2:11) and that, rather than conforming to the patterns of those around them, they are to stand out as people who are holy.

Rather than trusting in the folly of the cross, hyper-contextualization tries to dress up the gospel in worldly garb. Rather than making the messenger a plain and unprofitable servant, hyper-contextualization seeks to give the gospel messenger more influence than the gospel itself. At its root, it displays a lack of faith in the Bible. Iain Murray stated: "Herein lay the tragedy of the Church's approach to the world in the twentieth century. Hesitant now to proclaim authoritative truth, she solaced herself in the face of men's unwillingness to receive Christianity with the idea that the old "dogmatic approach" to evangelizing the earth was no longer legitimate. . . . Disbelief in Scripture lay hidden beneath professed charity and tolerance."[64]

SUFFERING ITSELF IS A GOSPEL WITNESS

Sometimes pragmatism is used to avoid suffering. But this, too, is a mark of dead orthodoxy. There are few things worse in the mind of dead orthodoxy than suffering for its faith. That is because its faith is choked out; it is dead. Thus, dead orthodoxy will try to make the gospel more attractive.

However, suffering itself is a gospel witness. Is it possible that God receives greater glory when His people suffer well for

---

64   Iain H. Murray, *The Puritan Hope* (Carlisle, PA: The Banner of Truth, 1971), 229.

His sake? For example, many people have been saved after hearing about Christians suffering for their faith. Justin Martyr is an example. He said about his pre-conversion days: "I myself, too, when I was delighting in the teachings of Plato and heard the Christians slandered and saw them fearless of death and of all things which are counted fearful, I understood."[65] In the footnote to this quote, Michael Green expounds on the context in which Justin was writing: "He understood from the way they met their deaths that the Christians could not be, as they were accused of being, living in wickedness and vice. But the impact of these deaths on him as a vindication of the doctrines they espoused is obvious."[66] In another place, Green declares that the suffering of Christians was the means for many converts in the early church: "The assurance and confidence of the Christians, who were quite willing to lose home, comfort, friends, and even life itself in propagating their cause, won its share of converts."[67]

Perhaps this is what Paul meant when he said, *That what has happened to me has really served to advance the gospel, so that it has become known throughout the whole imperial guard and to all the rest that my imprisonment is for Christ* (Philippians 1:13). The suffering of Paul even encouraged others to go out and share their faith with more boldness, meaning that more evangelism was happening on account of it (Philippians 1:14). How different such an approach is from our current one in which Christians in the West think that persecution and reproach can only bring shame to the gospel.

In the days of the early church, pagan religions were also willing to help the poor and set up institutions for social aid. Pagans, too, loved one another. Some were probably very nice

---

65   Michael Green, *Evangelism in the Early Church*, (Grand Rapids: Eerdmans, 2003), 200.

66   Ibid., 435.

67   Ibid., 176.

people, like many Buddhists, Muslims, and Roman Catholics are today. But why did Christianity see growth in the early centuries and not paganism? The Christians could not have offered material or social comforts because they had none, nor would it have been wise to broadcast themselves through such means. They could not have promised protection against enemies like many pagan religions could. In fact, the opposite was true. To become a Christian was to lose protection against enemies and to lose any social aid. These were not pragmatists. The only argument for pragmatism in the early Christian era would have been the miracles they performed, but even this cannot explain why Christians attracted followers since pagans had miracle workers as well.

The only explanation is their approach to evangelism. No one else in the world, including ethnic Jews, could match the way the Christians proclaimed the gospel, and it resulted in both converts and suffering. The two went hand in hand. Pagans leaving their religions for Christianity created "waves of desperation" throughout the empire, which only led to more persecution. Christian evangelism brought spiritual "destruction" to the other religions, and it was accomplished through the simple means of gospel proclamation and prayer. Even secular historians now admit this: "It was this result, destruction, that non-Christians of the time perceived as uniquely Christian; and it was this result which in turn gave so grave a meaning, from the pagan point of view as well as the Christian, to the successive waves of persecution."[68]

This is another reminder that anything that attempts to soften or hide the realities of the gospel is unworthy of Jesus Christ. Gospel proclamation is a means for converting sinners. But those who hear about Christians suffering on account of the gospel will be likely to inquire more deeply into the Christian

---

68 Ramsay MacMullen, *Christianizing the Roman Empire* (New Haven, CT: Yale University Press, 1984), 109.

faith and ask why they were willing to go through such reproach. At the very least, the sufferings of the Christian will generate more boldness in other Christians so that they then go out and share the gospel.

Using pragmatic measures in evangelism or church growth, as innocent as it may seem, cannot be done in good conscience since God's work is often mysterious and not necessarily according to any kind of set pattern. Sometimes evangelism will result in people being saved. Other times, the consequence will be terrible persecution, and after hearing about the Christians' response to this oppression, others may be drawn to Christ. The persecuted Christian may never know that his suffering motivates others to go share the gospel which in turn is used to save more people. But even if none are saved, the most important thing is that Christ's name is being preached, and hence, Christ receives glory.

Whether or not someone is saved, suffering for the sake of the gospel is a glorious testimony to the reality of God. So why are so many ministries and Christians reluctant to suffer? Why are so many ashamed when the lost are offended? Why are so many ashamed of losing their "good" reputation in the eyes of the world? Why do so many fear bad reviews on their websites? The main objectives of dead orthodoxy are to keep oneself safe from suffering and to be seen as reputable in the eyes of the world. It thinks this will cast more attractive light on Christ. Biblical testimony and church history show the opposite is true.

Paul addressed the same thing in 2 Corinthians 2:15-16: *For we are the aroma of Christ to God among those who are being saved and among those who are perishing, to one a fragrance from death to death, to the other a fragrance from life to life.* Paul has already acknowledged that evangelism helps spread *the fragrance of the knowledge of him everywhere* (2 Corinthians 2:14). Evangelism and, more specifically, the Christian who evangelizes, are like offerings of sweet incense to God. We give the gospel *to those who are being saved* and, likewise, *to those who are perishing*. When we evangelize, we please God regardless of whether the *one* is saved. We are *a fragrance from death to death* to those who are lost. The one evangelizing smells like death. The message itself is death. But what happens next marks the contrast between biblical evangelism and pragmatism. Biblical evangelism is sharing the gospel even if it only produces death. The one evangelizing will not change the gospel to make the odor more appealing. They will not try to spray it with pragmatic perfume or hide it under flesh-appealing paint. They will not dress it up in fancy garments. Biblical evangelism is knowing that only God can change a person's view of the gospel, and it is His sovereign will alone to do so. Our job is to share it.

On the other hand, as Paul mentioned one verse later, pragmatists will *peddle* the gospel to protect themselves against suffering. Such an approach chops it up in order to suppress its offence: *For we are not, like so many, peddlers of God's word, but as men of sincerity, as commissioned by God, in the sight of God we speak in Christ* (2 Corinthians 2:17). Anyone who deliberately keeps back the full gospel of God is gospel peddling, or pragmatizing, and they often do it out of fear of suffering.

HOW THE WEST WAS WON: THE HOLY SPIRIT

There is an abundance of compromise, timidity, worldliness, and sentimentality in the Christian world today. This is unacceptable. Have we not learned after two centuries of pragmatism that compromise does not work and that trying to appease the world has backfired? It is time to embrace being a mockery of the world and to rely on the Holy Spirit when we engage a hostile culture like ours. This was what won over Rome in the first four centuries after Christ's resurrection. Pragmatism did not do it. The prayer meetings, evangelism, faithfulness, and unwavering stances of the believers are what won over Rome, even if they were unattractive to the culture they lived in. This is what God used to change the world.

The parable of the soils gives us a sower who is simple and nameless (Mark 4:1-20). The seed he sowed was simply seed, yet it was effective when sown into fertile soil. The seed did not need to be painted a fancy color. It did not need to be pumped with strange chemicals. It was good enough, and so is the gospel. It is not the messenger but the power of God that gives the growth to seed that has not been tampered with. If our orthodoxy is dead, we will require something other than the help of the Holy Spirit.

Is this true of you? Is the gospel no longer enough? Because we lack power and unction from the Holy Spirit, have we been tempted to manufacture things as a way to help God out? We would never admit this on paper, but as we reach the end of this book, now is the time to face these questions honestly. Have we shrunk away from discussing hell, homosexuality, abortion, or any other topic that might be offensive to the unbeliever? Have we held back the whole counsel of God because we feared it would push someone away? Where have we compromised? Where have we been dead? Where have we been pragmatic? *"Come, let us return to the LORD; for he has torn us, that he may heal us; he has struck us down, and he will bind us up. After two days he will revive us; on the third day he will raise us up, that we may live before him"* (Hosea 6:1-2).

STUDY QUESTIONS

1. What are some examples of pragmatism you have seen in your local church or in the area where you live and serve?

2. Have you ever resorted to pragmatism as a way to make the gospel more palatable?

3. What is the line between pragmatism and healthy contextualization? Why is it so hard to discern at times?

4. Why is pragmatism so popular in evangelicalism today? Do you feel the problem is getting better or worse?

CONCLUSION

I n one of Jesus's more scathing denunciations, He said, *"Woe to you, scribes and Pharisees, hypocrites! For you are like white-washed tombs, which outwardly appear beautiful, but within are full of dead people's bones and all uncleanness"* (Matthew 23:27).

Historically, whitewashed tombs were a way to venerate the dead. They were meant to spruce up the receptacle of the corpse. The same can be said of dead orthodoxy. It is an attempt to prop up what is dead through custom, ritual, pomp, noise, and sham piety. It is an effort to appease the conscience by appealing to some nominal action such as saying a prayer, walking an aisle, or wearing a cross necklace, even when those actions do not mark the person's life in any profound way. Jesus said there are those who *outwardly appear beautiful, but within are full of dead people's bones and all uncleanness* (Matthew 23:27).

But the practice of whitewashing tombs also served as a warning. It marked off the tombs as a restricted area to prevent uncleanness for the person who would be exposed to the dead body. It was a cautionary measure for the people in the vicinity. We, too, can make use of this warning. Avoid dead orthodoxy.

Root it out and run from it. It has been around for a long time, and it is deadly and staining.

We should not avoid people caught up in this sin. The Bible says we should warn, encourage, and restore them, always keeping watch on ourselves and our own hearts, lest we, too, be tempted (Galatians 6:1). It is easy to point the finger at another person's deadness, but what about our own? Are we running on empty? Is our spiritual life dry and desertlike? Are we dead, perhaps? If so, what are we to do? What do we tell others to do? Turn to Jesus. Gaze once more upon Him. Consider the glories of the gospel and the inheritance we have in Christ. Call out to Him to save you. Cry to Him to awaken you. Christ is a Person. He hears you. He sees you.

WE NEED BALANCE

One of Satan's most successful tactics to defeat the Christian life is to employ extremes.[69] For example, if the doctrine of the Holy Spirit is taken to extremes of fanaticism and oddity, our reaction is then to deny the life of the Holy Spirit altogether. If certain groups see the devil in everything, others will respond by refusing to see him anywhere. If some groups say that every gift of the Holy Spirit is operative in every local church and at every period of the church, others will say that no gift of the Holy Spirit was intended to be operative after the age of the apostles. If some groups err toward legalism, the response is often antinomianism.

In this scenario, Satan wins both ways. In the one group, the most grotesque and fanatical events are passed off as the work of the Holy Spirit. In the other, men recoil in horror and deny the

---

69   This section has been influenced by Charles Leiter's paper, "Cessationism vs. Continuationism: An Error of Extremes."

miraculous gifts of the Holy Spirit altogether. Either way, Satan manages to partially discredit the work of the Holy Spirit and trick men into formulating their doctrinal positions in response to errors he introduced, not in the terms that the Bible sets forth.[70]

But the Scriptures reveal balance, especially regarding the Holy Spirit. Until the return of Christ, the church will be characterized by a general outpouring and manifestation of the Holy Spirit. This does not mean that these manifestations will be uniform at every time and place, since both biblically and historically, there are seasons of special activity on the part of the Holy Spirit. But the activity of the Holy Spirit is to mark the period between Pentecost and Christ's second coming, so we should expect to see the fruit of this in our lives and churches. This is one of the ways in which the *New Covenant* is new. There is a powerful outpouring of God's power on all His people, yet such special activity on the part of the Holy Spirit is according to God's sovereign will. Man does not manufacture it. We can neither dictate nor manipulate when or how God is going to reveal Himself in a unique way. It is not a science but a miracle. That God does reveal Himself through such special activity of the Holy Spirit is certain, and to appreciate this will help counteract certain influences of extremes.

We need this idea of balance regarding the Christian life as well. People typically swing from hot to cold on any given day. Christian affections, or inclinations, toward God, His ways, and His works, seem to come and go in all of us. While we are praying and reading the Bible, our hearts can glow with love for God. Thirty minutes later, we may be feeling resentment toward our spouse or boss, and by the end of the day, we may

---

70   Leiter, "Cessationism vs. Continuationism."

find ourselves dry, hard, and absent from all things spiritual. We have seemingly lost any lively engaging of the will toward God. It is easy to grow dark with despair. Conversely, if we can sustain a red-hot zeal for God over a lengthy period, we may find it easy to become Pharisaical toward those of lesser spiritual attainment. We begin to look down on such people. We become puffed up and proud. What happens next is inevitable: God humbles us by some circumstance, and He lets us fall.

The Christian life is one of ups and downs, so to understand this about ourselves is a way to maintain balance and perspective. You are hot now? See it as God's grace. Be humble. You are cold now? Do not despair, but rather seek the face of God, pursue spiritual disciplines, and wait until the fire returns.

The fact that the Scriptures use such language as *be filled with the Spirit* (Ephesians 5:18) and *do not grieve the Holy Spirit* (Ephesians 4:30) indicates that the presence of the Holy Spirit is more obvious in some seasons of life than in others. The Holy Spirit is always dwelling in the believer. That much does not change. But there are various levels or seasons of power, awareness, and fullness of the Holy Spirit in the life of the believer. There are seasons when the Holy Spirit manifests Himself in us in a way more powerful and obvious than in other seasons.

When stuck in the slough of despond, another thing to remember is that sorrow over our lack of God-directed emotion is itself a battering ram against dead orthodoxy. To feel sorrow over one's deadness means the deadness is already thawing. To feel sorrow is a type of warmth, not a result of coldness. It means we have tasted the joys of the living God, and we thirst for more of them. The fact that we regret our current condition is a mark of warm orthodoxy. Be encouraged by this, not discouraged. Consider the example of a tree. A living tree will bleed if you scar it deeply with a knife. This response is a sign of life and activity. Do the same thing to a dead tree, however, and nothing will happen. Sorrow and grief are signs of the Holy Spirit at work in a person's soul. Turn to Jesus, now, and let Him do His regenerative healing.

MORE REASON FOR OPTIMISM

It is a recognized fact that Presbyterian, Dutch Reformed, and Second London Baptist churches have in general been lacking in warm orthodoxy in the not-so-distant past. But, of late, there seems to be a concerted effort to change that among these same groups. This is a cause for serious optimism. This seems to be true for individuals as well. People are simply not buying the arguments that are coming from more hyper-cessationist camps. Admitting there is a problem is the first step to recovery. If dead orthodoxy is a problem in your life or denomination, confess it and turn to Jesus.

This is happening already in large swaths of the Western world. Many people in what have traditionally been called *dead* or *frozen* traditions are now preaching on the streets, ministering at abortion clinics, running for government offices, starting Christian schools, planting churches, teaching their kids the Scriptures, evangelizing their neighbors, and attending prayer meetings. Orthodoxy is heating up.

Jesus proved to be someone completely different from the people He called whitewashed tombs. He came to bring life and joy. In Him is rest and peace, not the drudgery of false religion. The sparkle of whitewashed tombs can never create the deep-seated, inward transformation that comes from the new birth that the gospel provides. Ultimately, this is what we need. *In him we have redemption through his blood, the forgiveness of our trespasses, according to the riches of his grace* (Ephesians 1:7).

Can these bones live? . . . O Lord GOD, you know (Ezekiel 37:3).

STUDY QUESTIONS

1. How has this book shaped the way you see the church today? How has it shaped the way you see yourself?

2. How has this book shaped the way you see the lost?

3. As we look at the church today, where do we find areas to be optimistic? What areas need improvement?

4. Where have you been imbalanced in your theology or Christian living?

APPENDIX

HYPER-CESSATIONISM AND THE "WESTMINSTER CONFESSION OF FAITH"

In a series of articles I wrote for Reformation21, I maintained that the word *cessationism* needs to be used in the way it was given to us by the Westminster divines. I argued that the tightened, more restricted version of cessationism as espoused by many in cessationist camps today merits the term *hyper-cessationism* since it would be disingenuous to use it in a way that is more hardline and rigid than how Westminster originally used it. This appendix seeks to prove these points.

REVELATION AND THE SUFFICIENCY OF SCRIPTURE

The crux of the debate centers around the concept of revelation. While both sides believe God has given us an infallible, inspired, and entirely unique revelation in the Holy Scriptures, the hyper-cessationist camp has insisted that no further forms of revelation are now available. This is in opposition to the majority Puritan and Covenanter view, however. Historians such as J. I. Packer, Garnet Howard Milne, Michael Haykin, and Vern Poythress have either implied or expressed agreement with the assertion that the Puritans and Covenanters believed in a type of revelation that continued to be operative in the church, such as that which is communicated through dreams, visions, prophetic impulses, and even angelic communication. Such revelation is not inspired or infallible in the same way the Holy Scriptures are, nor does it give us any new doctrine or ethics. It is circumstantial or personal in nature, and because it is given to non-apostolic individuals prone to sin and biases, it is always to be checked against Scripture. Ideally, it will even work in tandem with Scripture – but it is revelation, nonetheless. Dean R. Smith, in a paper published by *Westminster Theological Journal* (2001), stated: "The strict cessationist perspective of Warfield and others is a limited perspective on what the reformers and their descendants believed and practiced. If Knox, the Scottish Presbyterians, and the Covenanters were living today in the same manner that they did in the 1500s and 1600s, we would be forced to classify them more with the continuationists than the cessationists."[71]

I have provided many primary source examples in prior articles, but consider two more. The first is a statement by Peter Martyr Vermigli (1499-1562), a Reformer and close friend of Calvin's. In his *Philosophical Works*, after a lengthy section on Augustine and Cyprian's revelatory dreams, Vermigli stated, "Therefore, a good and lawful attention to dreams is not to be forbidden; the godly are permitted to pray that they may be instructed even in their dreams."[72]

John Flavel (1627-1691), writing in the Reformed tradition over one hundred years later, stated the following in question nine of his exposition of the "Westminster Shorter Catechism":

---

71   Dean Smith, "The Scottish Presbyterians and Covenanters: A Continuationist Experience in a Cessationist Theology," *Westminster Theological Journal* 63, no. 1 (2001), 44.

72   Peter Vermigli, *Philosophical Works: On the Relation of Philosophy to Theology,* trans. and ed. Joseph McClelland (Burford, England: Davenant, 2018), 168.

"Q. But if a man have a voice, a vision, or a dream, seeming to hint the secret will of God, may he not obey it?

"A. Yes; if it be consonant to the revealed will of God in the word."

Both of these views accord with John Knox's statements in a sermon he delivered on August 19, 1565: "I dare not deny (lest that in so doing, I should be injurious to the giver,) but that *God hath revealed unto me secrets unknown to the world*; and also, that he hath made my tongue a trumpet to forewarn realms and nations; yea, certain great revelations of mutations and changes, when no such things were feared, nor yet were appearing; a portion whereof cannot the world deny (be it never so blind) to be fulfilled, and the rest, alas!" (italics mine)[73]

To call Vermigli, Knox, and Flavel heavyweights in the Reformed world would be an understatement, yet they clearly approve of lower forms of revelation for the purpose of personal or even national guidance and edification. Such revelation was never viewed as competing with the sufficiency of Scripture, but personal revelation through dreams, visions, or impulses, to name a few examples, was popular enough to be mentioned approvingly, albeit with understandable cautions.

WHAT ABOUT THE "WESTMINSTER CONFESSION"?

This brings us to the "Westminster Confession of Faith." Considering what has just been stated, how do we understand the *cessationist clause* in Chapter 1? Does this close the door to revelation from God, even if it is of a lower order than the type of revelation given to us in the Scriptures?

The answer is no. When the confession states "those former ways of God's revealing His will unto His people being now

---

73   John Knox, from a sermon preached August 19, 1565, Bibleexplore.com, accessed December 22, 2024, https://godrules.net/library/knox/15knox9.htm

ceased," the earlier context demonstrates that what is being spoken of here is the need for special revelation regarding salvation. We are told that natural revelation and the light of nature can give us certain insights about God, "yet are they not sufficient to give that knowledge of God, and of His will, *which is necessary unto salvation*" (italics mine) (1.1). This section deals with salvation and the revelation required for it. Only Holy Scripture can reveal to us what a man must do to be saved. The Scriptures are therefore *most necessary.*

But this is not the same thing as saying God does not communicate to His church in other ways, so long as they are consistent and even working in tandem with the Holy Scriptures, such as the Lord appeared to do with Knox. Westminster emphasized here that the Holy Scriptures are foundational, since anything communicated through dreams, visions, or prophetic impulses must be checked against it. This lower type of revelation, which the divines seemed to be comfortable with, in no way goes beyond Christ, but rather points back to Him as He is found in the Scriptures. The Scriptures are our presupposition for all religious epistemology and phenomena. The Bible is the first and primary source from which the Christian should seek guidance.

Commenting on this section of the "WCF," Milne notes, "Means by which God had once communicated the divine will *concerning salvation*, such as dreams, visions, and the miraculous gifts of the Spirit, were said to be no longer applicable. However, many of the authors of the 'WCF' accepted that 'prophecy' continued in their time, and a number of them apparently believed that disclosure of God's will through dreams, visions, and angelic communication remained possible."[74] Later, Milne states, "The written Word of God was fully capable of showing the way of 'salvation' in its wider scope as either temporal

---

74   Milne, *Westminster Confession*, xv.

or eternal deliverance."[75] Thus, to assert that the "WCF" 1.1 is here expressing something beyond the scope of salvation would seem to go beyond its intention. The divines believed that immediate revelation had ceased but that a lower, mediate form of revelation continued.

This idea of a lower order of revelation can be seen in "WCF" 1.6, where we are told, "Nothing at any time is to be added [to the Scriptures], whether by new revelations of the Spirit, or traditions of men." The confession here implies that *new revelations of the Spirit* are a live (even if infrequent) possibility but that such revelations must not add to the Scriptures.

This is exactly the type of revelation that we have been seeing in the historical data. It is circumstantial in nature, in the sense of God dispensing revelation for the sake of certain circumstances, whether personal or national. It is also always in accordance with and even working through the Holy Scriptures. But such revelation never adds to the Scriptures since it never communicates any new doctrine or ethics. Smith, in the *WTJ* article mentioned above, agrees: "The phrase *whether by new revelations of the Spirit* in the "WCF" 1.6 is a recognition within the Westminster Assembly that such extraordinary revelation may have existed but that it was not equal in authority with the Scriptures. In other words, there may be new revelations of the Spirit, but the only infallible rule of faith and life is the Word of God in the Scriptures."[76]

Such a reading is consistent with the views of certain participants of the Westminster Assembly, especially Samuel Rutherford, George Gillespie, and William Bridge. We have also seen that such an idea is not foreign to the seventeenth-century Reformed worldview in general. Such a reading also means that we should not outrightly reject *traditions of men,* which makes sense, because the "WCF" is itself a tradition. Thus, it is more

---

75   Milne, *Westminster Confession,* xvi
76   Smith, "Scottish Presbyterians," 44.

accurate to understand the "Westminster Confession" here as rejecting not revelations or traditions per se but those revelations or traditions which would add to Scripture. The kind of revelation given by dreams, visions, and prophetic impulses are limited to certain occasions and circumstances. This is why Knox, Vermigli, and Flavel were willing to accept them as options while at the same time holding to the sufficiency of Scripture.

The other noteworthy section of the confession is 1.10. It states: "The Supreme Judge, by which all controversies of religion are to be determined, and all decrees of councils, opinions of ancient writers, doctrines of men, and private spirits, are to be examined, and in whose sentence we are to rest, can be no other but the Holy Spirit speaking in the Scripture." It is the phrase, *private spirits*, that we will look at here. Milne does not think this is a reference to private revelation, but Byron Curtis, in an article in the *Westminster Theological Journal*, compellingly argues that the seventeenth-century understanding of the phrase *private spirits* was "private revelation, not personal opinion."[77] He came to his conclusion by researching how the phrase was used in the literature of that time. This would substantiate what we have already seen in the confession, and it would also be consistent with the viewpoints of certain of the divines and Reformers.

Although the divines gave us the confession from which we derive the term *cessationism*, we see how nuanced and complex the situation is. It is no wonder that the same people who penned the cessationist clause in Chapter 1 also gave us this in "WCF" 5.3: "God, in his ordinary providence, maketh use of means, yet is free to work without, above, and against them, at his pleasure."

---

77   Byron Curtis, "'Private Spirits' in 'The Westminster Confession' of Faith §1.10 and in Catholic-Protestant Debate (1588–1652)," *Westminster Theological Journal* 58 (Fall 1996), 258.

CONCLUSION

There is a difference between historic cessationism and the type of cessationism that is being popularized today. Most people are unaware of this distinction, which is why it is important that we teach the differences between the two. No one wants to quench the Spirit, but I fear this updated version of cessationism is doing just that. My critics want to say the divines and Covenanters got it wrong on this one, which is fine if they think so, but my request is that they produce another term, such as *hyper-cessationism*, to better categorize their novel position.

BIBLIOGRAPHY

Baxter, Richard. *A Christian Directory*. London: 1673.

Bridge, William. *The Works of the Rev. Bridge*. Vol. 1. London: Thomas Tegg, 1845.

Bunyan, John. *Grace Abounding to the Chief of Sinners*. Reprint of the 1905 The Religious Tract Society edition, Project Gutenberg, 2013. https://www.gutenberg.org/files/654/654-h/654-h.htm.

_____. *The Pilgrim's Progress*. Project Gutenberg, 2021. https://www.gutenberg.org/files/131/131-h/131-h.htm.

_____. *The Straight Gate: The Great Difficulty of Going to Heaven*. London: 1676.

Calvin, John. *The First Epistle of Paul to the Corinthians*. Translated by John W. Fraser. Grand Rapids, MI: Eerdmans, 1960.

_____. *Institutes of the Christian Religion*. Edited by John T. McNeill. Philadelphia: Westminster Press, 1960.

Chesterman, A. de M. "The Journals of Daniel Brainerd and of William Carey," *The Baptist Quarterly* 19 (1961–62).

Curtis, Byron. "'Private Spirits' in 'The Westminster Confession' of Faith §1.10 and in Catholic-Protestant Debate (1588–1652)." *Westminster Theological Journal* 58 (Fall 1996).

Gillespie, George. *The Works of George Gillespie*, Vol. 2. Edited by David Meek. Edmonton: SWRB, 1991.

Green, Michael. *Evangelism in the Early Church*. Grand Rapids: Eerdmans, 2003.

Grudem, Wayne. *The Gift of Prophecy in the New Testament and Today*. rev. ed. Wheaton, IL: Crossway, 2000.

Haykin, Michael, A. G. *The Missionary Fellowship of William Carey*. Sanford, FL: Reformation Trust Publishing, 2018.

Hodge, Charles. *A Commentary on 1 & 2 Corinthians*. Carlisle, PA: Banner of Truth, 1974.

Howie, John. *The Scots Worthies*. 1870. Reprint, Carlisle, PA: Banner of Truth, 1995.

Josephus, Flavius. *War of the Jews*, in *The Genuine Works of Flavius Josephus, the Jewish Historian*. Translated by Henry St. John Thackeray. Cambridge, MA: Harvard University Press, 1950.

"The Life of John Flavel." *The Works of John Flavel*, Vol. 1. 1691. Reprint, Carlisle, PA: Banner of Truth, 1968.

Lloyd-Jones, Martyn. *Revival*. Wheaton, IL: Crossway, 1987.

MacArthur, John. "Theology of Sleep." In *Evangelism*. Nashville: Thomas Nelson, 2011.

MacMullen, Ramsay. *Christianizing the Roman Empire*. New Haven: Yale University Press, 1984.

Mather, Cotton. *Parentator: Memoirs of Remarkables in the Life and the Death of the Ever-Memorable Dr. Increase Mather.* Boston: B. Green, 1724.

Milne, Garnet Howard. *The Westminster Confession of Faith and the Cessation of Special Revelation.* Eugene, OR: Paternoster, 2007.

Morgan, J. Vyrnwy. *The Welsh Religious Revival, 1904–5: A Retrospect and a Criticism.* London: Chapman & Hall, 1909.

Murray, Iain H. *Puritan Hope.* Carlisle, PA: Banner of Truth, 1971.

_____. *Revival & Revivalism.* Carlisle, PA: Banner of Truth, 1994.

Owen, John. *Exposition on the Book of Hebrews.* Edinburgh: Banner of Truth, 1991.

Plato. *Plato: Collected Dialogues.* Edited by Hamilton & Cairns. Translated by P. Shorey. Princeton, NJ: Random House, 1963.

Rutherford, Samuel. *A Survey of the Spiritual Antichrist.* London: 1648.

Ryle, J. C. *Practical Religion.* Newberry, FL: Logos, 2022.

Smith, Dean. "The Scottish Presbyterians and Covenanters: A Continuationist Experience in a Cessationist Theology." *Westminster Theological Journal* 63, no. 1 (2001): 39–63.

Sproul, R. C. *Essential Truths of the Christian Faith.* Carol Stream, IL: Tyndale House Publishers, 1992.

Spurgeon, Charles. *Pictures from Pilgrim's Progress.* London: Counted Faithful, 1903. Tertullian. "On Idolatry." *The Ante-Nicene Fathers.* Edited by Alexander Roberts and James Donaldson. Peabody, MA: Hendrickson, 1994.

Vermigli, Peter. *Philosophical Works: On the Relation of Philosophy to Theology.* Translated and edited by Joseph McClelland. Burford, England: Davenant, 2018.

Whitefield, George. *The Revived Puritan: The Spirituality of George Whitefield.* Edited by

Michael Haykin. Peterborough, Ontario: Joshua Press, 2000.

Whyte, Alexander. *Bunyan Characters.* Reprint of the 1893 edition, Project Gutenberg, 2005. https://www.gutenberg.org/files/1885/1885-h/1885-h.htm

ABOUT THE AUTHOR

Ryan Denton was a pastor on the Navajo Reservation before serving in the Vanguard Presbyterian Church as an evangelist. He has degrees from The Southern Baptist Theological Seminary, St. John's College, the University of New Mexico, and he has a ThM from Puritan Reformed Theological Seminary.

He is a prolific writer, and his works have appeared at Reformation Heritage Books, Reformation 21, Desiring God, Founders Ministries, The Confessional Presbyterian, and others.

He and his wife, Tasha, live in Texas with their three sons.

www.presbypreacher.com